Preface t
"My Redeemer Lives:

"My Redeemer Lives"… the words come from the ...
book of Job. The early saint and patriarch resolved to
believe that his Redeemer continues to exist and would
eventually take his victorious position among His people.

> "As for me, I know that my Redeemer lives, and at
> the last He will take His stand on the earth." (Job
> 19:25)

This verse was inexplicably recalled and shouted amidst
the hardest time of the life of my precious wife, Carol R.
Quinn.

The "R" stands for Rookstool, Carol's family name…
which explains her beloved nickname "Rook". That has
been Carol's handle from the time I met her in the
summer of 1974. We encountered each other as we
worked summer jobs at the Atlantic City Race Track
supporting our college years. We became instant friends,
then sweethearts and at the writing of this book, husband
and wife for 34 wonderful years of marriage. Since those
days, Carol has always been my best friend!

The book's title comes from the expression of this faith-
filled woman in the middle of an ordeal that changed our
lives forever. The year was 2009. We had been married
at the time for 25 years. This is the true story about the
events which began in early August on a Colorado
vacation.

As Carol went through her trial in the late summer/early
fall of 2009, she was the epitome of a faith warrior who
fought with everything she could muster to meet the
shocking set of circumstances she faced. She was full of

grace and love, even though at times there was plenty of panic and concern over what was happening. As she often said, "I just want to get better."

Maybe as you hear her/our story, this book may help when life events seem to be spinning out of control and all you want is a handle to hold onto or a compass setting to mark the course forward. It is our hope this true story may help you see how God helped us in the most difficult time of our lives.

So we present "Redeemer Lives: Rook's Book".

George J. Quinn
2018

Foreword

Thank you so much for choosing to read this book. Our purpose in writing it was to glorify the Lord, to help others who may find themselves and their lives turned upside down, and to demonstrate the power of faith and friends.

The format of the book is unique. It is comprised of my narrative of the events that transpired as I remember them. However, due to my brain injury, much of what occurred was recounted to me by those friends, family members, and caregivers who surrounded me during this journey. In addition, my husband kept a daily journal of my situation and also started writing daily reflections of this time entitled "morning thoughts". As you follow us through the days, weeks, and months, the reading will not be smooth as you will be hearing from a variety of sources and multiple vantage points. We ask your indulgence, as the staccato style is a perfect representation of life surrounding an incident of this nature.

> Blessed be God, even the Father of our Lord Jesus Christ, the Father of mercies, and the God of all comfort; Who comforts us in all our tribulation, that we may be able to comfort them which are in any trouble, by the comfort wherewith we ourselves are comforted of God. (I Corinthans1:3-4 KJV)

Carol R. Quinn
2017

Acknowledgements

It is impossible to acknowledge everyone who was instrumental in bringing this book to the form and format you are about to read. Whenever one begins to thank people, he or she invariably forgets to mention someone of import. However, the following individuals were asked to read and edit the "manuscript" in its original state and assist us in making it available to the public. We are very thankful for their assistance, input, and friendship.

Ricky Kearney
D.J. Schrag
Roseann Stollenwerk
John P. Quinn

Table of Contents

Chapter 1 - "Trouble in the Rockies"

Lying in the hospital bed in the emergency room with an excruciating headache was a sufficiently scary experience for me at this stage of my otherwise routine life! However when the discussion of transporting me to Jefferson Hospital in Philadelphia, Pennsylvania by HELICOPTER, amidst an August thunderstorm, in the dark was broached, scary took on a whole new dimension! I attempted to explain to the attending physician if the symptoms that brought me to the hospital did not kill me, the impending helicopter ride might just do the job.

Who knew that thunderstorm would turn out to be my saving grace? The Lord! The same Lord who had brought me to this place, who would see me through blindness, immobility, consternation of my physicians, therapy, recovery and restoration! The Lord who holds us and the world in the palm of His caring hands! Because of that storm, I rode to Jefferson in the back of an ambulance that fortunately never left the ground!

Whoever said hindsight is 20/20 is a genius! That aborted helicopter ride was the culmination of a series of small events that, in retrospect, seem quite connected and obvious. At the time, however, we were far too engrossed in the beauty that is Estes Park, Colorado, and the spiritual oasis that is Wind River Ranch. If you ever have the opportunity to visit Wind River Ranch, do. If you don't have the opportunity, make one!

Nestled in the Colorado Rockies, Estes Park is a breathtaking and almost indescribable spot. Estes Park is the base camp for Rocky Mountain National Park (RMNP). Templed mountains with evergreen spires edge the beautiful daily blue sky. Every turn of the road presents a new breathtaking vista of Rocky Mountain beauty. Thousands of visitors stream into Estes Park en route to the eastern gate of one of the most popular national parks in America. So, especially in the middle of the summer, the town is full of ten speed bikers, kayak rowers and mountain-trail hikers.

George and I had the pleasure of visiting there once before with George's twin brother, John and his wife, Carol for our joint 20th anniversaries. (Of course twin brothers who both married Carols and are both pastors would get married in the same year!) We were amazed at God's handiwork and blessed by the ministry of Wind River Ranch. During that visit we purposed in our hearts to return, Lord willing, with our dear friends, Frank and Debbie Holliday, and their three children, Ian, Jared, and Alyssa.

Wind River Ranch is a remarkable setting and holds out remarkable experiences for anyone, but especially for families. The road from Estes Park to the Wind River Ranch is a breathtaking ride. The drive is due south on the picturesque Route 7 that runs along the eastern edge of the Rocky Mountain National Park.

The ranch which was originally settled in the 1880s is across the street from RMNP and the majestic Long's Peak whose 14,256-foot crown stands heads and shoulders over the surrounding mountains. It is a horse ranch and camp. We were excited to share the experience with these friends on our return trip. Upon arrival at the ranch, George, Frank, and I decided to take a drive to Trail Ridge Road.

My name is Carol R. Quinn. This story is the story of the most important journey of my life; a journey that brought me face to face with my Savior. Most of my version of this journey was recounted to me by my husband, George.

7

Along with being the love of my life, brother in Christ, and caregiver/inspiration throughout this time in our lives, he was able to keep a journal of the events that transpired. In April of 2009, we had just celebrated our 25th wedding anniversary. George had been a pastor for 21 years and a physics teacher for 29 years. I worked at a local college... helping students with special needs in the Learning Access Program at Stockton State College, now Stockton University. Prior to my years at Stockton, I had a 21-year career in banking. But I digress... back to Trail Ridge Road and George's first journal entry.

Carol

Day 1 – Sunday, August 2, 2009

This was the first day that there was any hint of a problem. We had spent four days in Estes Park, Colorado and had a lot of fun with no problems. On Sunday, our friend Frank, Carol & I took a ride into Rocky Mountain National Park. We drove along Trail Ridge Road. We stopped at an elevation of slightly over 12,000 feet to check out the wildlife - marmots and elk. Carol got out of the car to get a closer look at the resting elk and suffered a sharp, piercing pain in her head. She took a Tylenol Sinus Multi-symptom pain reliever. We came down to the ranch where we were staying at 9000 feet and Carol was fine.

Day 2 – Monday, August 3, 2009

An uneventful morning – we hung around the ranch. Carol started to get a piercing headache toward the end of the day... she took an Advil.

That night she was uncomfortable all night. She slept on the sofa in our room instead of the bed.

Day 3 – Tuesday, August 4, 2009

We went to an urgent care facility called the Timberline Clinic in Estes Park. Her blood pressure was 184/112. They did a CT scan and said everything looked fine. The doctor said that Carol might have a bad case of altitude sickness. He gave us a script for a diuretic and said that the pills should bring down her blood pressure. We went to the Rocky Mountain Pharmacy in Estes Park and received hydrochlorothiazide 25 mg. He said if she had the headaches again, to come down to Estes Park (5800 feet) and after she felt better to go back up. He said that if she came down to Estes and she still had the headaches to go to an even lower elevation, perhaps Boulder or Ft. Collins. He said if the headaches continued we would have to go to a hospital. We returned to the hotel in which we stayed in Estes Park prior to the ride to Wind River. Carol was fine.

Day 4 – Wednesday, August 5, 2009

We went whitewater rafting in Ft. Collins (below 5,000 feet). We had a good time and Carol had no headaches. After rafting, we went back up to the ranch. Carol took a shower and however when she bent over to dry her hair, the pain came back. The ranch staff graciously allowed us stay in a house in Estes Park and the headache was better (2 out of 10 on a pain scale).

I have been blessed with relatively good health for the majority of my life. I also have, in my opinion, a relatively high threshold of pain. These headaches were piercing. They came suddenly and were exacerbated with any movement of my head. It was like nothing I had ever experienced. For that reason, I assumed they were somehow related to the elevation and the visit to the clinic seemed to confirm that assumption. This trip was the trip-of-a-lifetime for all of us and I did NOT want to be the cause of its untimely ending.

Carol

Day 5 – Thursday, August 6, 2009

Thursday… we stayed at the house at Estes Park and did laundry. Carol was feeling better. We went up to the ranch to watch a show the kids performed – Carol was fine. We ate dinner, walked out of the dining hall, and Carol's headache returned.

We then drove down to the house in Estes Park following the protocol to go to a lower elevation. We got there and the headache would not go away. We decided to drive that night to Ft. Collins. It was after midnight and after an unsuccessful attempt, we did find a place to stay. It was a Days Inn that was five minutes from the hospital. Carol was feeling okay.

Day 6 – Friday, August 7, 2009

In the morning, Carol was fine. I drove back to the ranch leaving Carol at the hotel. The trip from Ft. Collins to the Wind River Ranch is over an hour of driving up through the front range of the Rockies. I arrived at the ranch and quickly packed up the few things we had left there. I said goodbye to the staff - giving them an update on Carol's condition. Everyone there was so concerned for Carol and promised to keep her in prayer. I got back in the car and quickly traveled to Ft. Collins.

I called the doctor at the Timberline Clinic and told him what happened & asked if he thought she could fly home to Philadelphia on Saturday. He said he thought Carol would be okay for the flight.

Day 7 – Saturday, August 8, 2009

We drove to the Denver Airport with the Hollidays. We were all concerned about Carol. We all flew home to Philadelphia and Carol seemed fine. She was a little sensitive to the light.

George

Despite the fact my traveling companions perceived me to be fine, I was not really. I vaguely remember the events described in George's journal, but my actual remembrance of the time in the Estes Park home and the Days Inn is misty and replete with large gaps. The fact that I allowed George to "pack up" our things at the ranch is one indication that I was in distress! I do not remember the flight home, the drive home or the arrival home.

11

As we traveled from Colorado back home to New Jersey, we had no idea of what lay ahead of us over the next six months, or the next six years.

Carol

Chapter 2 - "Things Get Dark"

Our flight landed in Philadelphia on Saturday night, August 8th. We drove home, started to unpack and went about our normal routine. That routine included church on Sunday. The fact that I did not go to church that Sunday morning is also an indication that all was not well. I try not to miss church services. And I believe this is where we started the story, my RIDE to Jefferson, not my FLIGHT!

Carol

Day 8 – (Day 1 @ Thomas Jefferson University Hospital) Sunday, August 9, 2009

Sunday morning, Carol was putting on her makeup and when she finished putting on her lip-liner, she couldn't replace the cap. She knew something was wrong. She looked at the television and she couldn't follow the scroll at the bottom of the screen. She called her friend, Debbie, and they went to the Urgent Care center near English Creek, five miles from our home. The staff there said they didn't have the kind of scanning equipment she would need so she would have to go to a hospital. I joined them at this point. We went to AtlantiCare Mainland Division in Galloway Township, New Jersey. They did a CT scan and found blood on the right side of her brain and recommended that she go right up to Jefferson Neuroscience in Philadelphia. We arrived at Jefferson on Sunday night. The only symptoms Carol was presenting were an inability to perceive depth and slight mental confusion.

George

What I recall of this trip is very minimal. I do recall my friend, Kelly, from my days as a teller at First Union Bank who is now a nurse coming to my room and comforting me before the ride to Jefferson.

What are the chances! Not chance when you are related to the God of the Universe! Not only would I see Kelly that evening, but she would also be with me at Betty Bacharach Rehabilitation Center during my many days of rehab.

I don't remember getting into the ambulance, the ride to Philadelphia, the arrival at Jefferson, or the admittance process. What I do remember however, is a big, dark room, being cold, and then a wonderful, soft-spoken woman, a neurological intensive care nurse named Pat, who made me warm with blankets and comforted by her very presence. There was also a male nurse named Nick; he and George became good friends over the next several days.

I could never capture in words the importance the staff at Jefferson (and hospitals like it) played in my recovery. From this first encounter through 25 days of in-patient care, they were a blessing. I hope and pray they know the part they all play in the lives of the patients who pass through those doors every day. I also hope they know how very much appreciated each and every deed they routinely do is. And I know the Lord will bless them for the care and comfort they give to all.

I remember George arriving at the big room and the joy I felt and always feel at the sight of him - well almost always! I remember the relief of being told I would probably need a small amount of physical therapy and then be on my way, and the relief of having George there to help me to the bathroom!

I remember nestling into the comfortable bed in the big dark room and slipping into a comforting sleep thinking the worst of this was behind us...

Carol

The next few days would be the longest of my life. We had no idea... no expectations. That is God's mercy I guess, because if we knew what was coming, it would have been worse.

During this time, there was a staff member who became a good friend to me. His name is Nick Lucenko. Nick was an excellent nurse for Carol and kept me informed on what "the white coats" were doing to treat Carol on her case. Nick and I were also Philadelphia Phillies fans... so one of the few connections to what was going on outside the Jefferson Neuroscience Hospital was the updates Nick would pass along on how the Phillies were doing. "The Phils" won the World Series in 2008... and then in 2009, they signed several big names to try to repeat the feat. They were cruising along in first place at that time, and Nick and I were happy for that pleasant distraction. Nick was so thoughtful.

After Carol was in the hospital bed for several days, Nick got the women in the department to help him give Carol a "Spa Day." At least that's how it was billed. They washed Carol's hair and blow dried it into a nice style. She felt good to have her "makeover".

George

15

Day 9 – (Day 2 @ Thomas Jefferson University Hospital)
Monday, August 10, 2009

Jefferson Neuroscience had Carol take a MRI early Monday morning. At that point the MRI showed no evidence of stroke or infarction. The first diagnosis was that the blood on the right side of the brain might be causing the tissue to become irritated which might account for the symptoms. The call was, if this is all it is, the brain would likely eventually reabsorb the blood and the symptoms should go away.

Day 10 – (Day 3 @ Thomas Jefferson University Hospital)
Tuesday, August 11, 2009

Carol's symptoms continue to get worse. She is becoming weaker in her left arm and leg. Her eyes are starting to gaze right and she is seeing less and less. The doctors order Carol to be brought down for more CT Scans.

The doctors are a little confused because even though Carol is presenting stroke-like symptoms, there is still no sign of stroke on the scans. It is Tuesday night and her left arm is becoming more lifeless and her vision is down to seeing colors and shadows. She can see a flashlight that is shining directly into her eye.

The doctors decide to treat her for a wide array of possible causes of her deteriorating condition. They believe that maybe she has something wrong with the blood vessels in her brain. They believe it might be vasculitis, vasospasms or some kind of constricting of the brain's vascular tissue. They

16

start a steroid treatment to reduce any inflammations and fight off possible vasospasms.

On the night shift, they start Carol on what is called a Triple H therapy (**H**ypertension – maintaining slightly higher blood pressure, **H**ypervolumia – maintaining high blood volume, and **H**emodilution – decreasing the cells and solids in blood by a continued influx of fluids). This therapy is a common treatment for patients following a sub-arachnoid hemorrhage (SAH). Her slightly increased blood pressure will allow for increased blood perfusion to all areas of her brain.

DJ Schrag - A friend's recollection (George's long-time friend and former student - a real brother!)

"Guys, feel free to add, subtract, edit or even omit as you see fit. Just the process of doing this was meaningful to me, even if it never sees the light of day..."

I must confess, I was not very reflective during the time of Carol's initial brain injury. More to the point, I was deeply shaken to see my dear friend in that condition. It wasn't difficult to obey the scriptural command to bear my brother and sister's burden (Galatians 6)...I had no choice. I could no more distance myself from the pain of what was happening than I could make myself fly. It simply wasn't an option.

Through the years, it has been my honor to walk with George and Carol through times both good and bad and sometimes ugly. Through all of that, we were always us. George was George: gracious, logical, fun, etc. Carol was Carol (well, really, Carol was Rookie): articulate, insightful, compassionate, funny, etc. I was me: the one

17

*they let hang around and call them friends (if you know them, you know what I mean), probably because I am one of the few that know the words to the Beatles **White Album**, and George can sing better than.*

Those early days at Jefferson Neuroscience were different. George was still George, and I was still me, but Carol wasn't Carol. [As I pondered my contribution to this book, I wondered which recollection would be the first to put a lump in my throat. I now have my answer, as I type through welled-up eyes]. This initial realization, and the mystery of the future (would Carol ever be the Rookie I knew again?) were something for which I was completely unprepared. I had no experience to draw on.

Never did I doubt our Savior's sovereignty, nor His power to heal, but there were times that I was simply too caught up in the storm to remember these life and hope-sustaining realities. Then, as He always does, the Lord reminded me that He is good, and that He has a perfect plan for His kids! Whether Carol would ever be the person she used to be was not the point. "The Big Guy's got this" was the point! As much as this hit us all out of the blue, it was carefully planned by the all-knowing, all-powerful Creator of time and space! He and He alone would work it out for the good!

Now it's only fair to confess, lest anyone mistake me for a better man than I am, that my experience of confidence in God's sovereignty was during my best moments. Much of my thoughts were much more surreal, if not downright bleak. "Could this really be happening", I asked myself frequently?! We had no choice but to walk by faith, and frankly, I didn't like it. Couldn't we just have some small reminder that Carol was going to be Carol again?!

Then it came: As one of the amazing nurses at Jefferson was doing a standard mental status exam, Carol clearly said "I know my Redeemer lives!" George and I looked at each other with what, I believe, was a combination of excitement, thankfulness, hope and encouragement, to name just a few of the complexity of feelings flooding us. There, for that brief moment, was our Carol! Six plus years later, that simple truth uttered by my stricken friend still brings everything into perspective! Despite this most violent of storms, "My Anchor Holds!" Ever will it hold!!

I believe one of the reasons God allows us to live in the broken/fallen/decaying world is so that we can experience Him at a depth that only suffering can prepare us to appreciate. Nobody appreciates a life-preserver quite like someone drowning. Looking back at this experience with George and Carol has taken me deeper into what it means to trust, and walk by faith despite what my eyes insist is happening. I've also noticed that it's made me appreciate the unique and amazing person that, by God's amazing grace, Carol is. She likely wouldn't know it, and in fact it only occurs to me now as I write this, but I also take just a little more joy in her wit and the frequent manifestations of her significant intelligence than I did before. Given how personal and intimate Jesus is, I'm sure He used this situation to teach many people an assortment of lessons. He showed me a little clearer picture of both the degree of brokenness in this world (that something like this could happen) and the beauty of the sweet fellowship with which I'm blessed in having the honor to walk with both George and Carol! To them, and ultimately our Lord, I'm humbly thankful for the invitation to share these thoughts!

David Joseph Schrag, LCSW

Day 11 – (Day 4 @ Thomas Jefferson University Hospital)
Wednesday, August 12, 2009

Carol's vision goes to zero; she can't see anything. Her left arm is paralyzed. The doctors say that they are treating her for everything they think it might be and we would have to let the medicine start to get a handle on the actual problem. Dr. Will Neil tells me that he believes that Carol has a better than 50% chance of seeing again. The staff tells me if she is going to regain her sight, it will return the same way it left. In other words, she will first see light and then shadows and eventually her vision might become clear again. I prayed for God to bring Carol's sight back, depending on His ability to restore what He created. I remember thinking how helpless we all were, including the doctors and we waited for God to heal.

George

The Lord is infinite in mercy and knowledge. I have NO remembrance of this time. Unlike my dear husband, who thought a better than 50% chance of my seeing again was good news, I would probably have seen (pardon the pun) the glass as half empty at that point! And that is precisely why He had me in the dark and my husband and Himself at the helm!

Carol

Patti Meredith, a sister-in-Christ and a source of encouragement and amusement to this day...

I remember my daughters, Kelsey and Cori and I visiting Carol several times in the hospital in Philadelphia. On one visit we brought an angel as a gift for her.

20

At that point in time – Carol could not see and so Pastor George described it to her. As Carol thanked us – she was looking in the opposite direction from where we were sitting – which broke my heart. She was blind and could not even raise her hand – we were so sad and we prayed and prayed for a miracle and a complete recovery.

By the next visit I had decided that Carol and George were there because someone in the hospital desperately needed to be saved, and God knew only Carol and George had the faith to witness to the staff by their love for God and their complete trust in Him. However, we were still afraid... so I asked Pastor George – "Are you scared?" and his answer is my greatest memory... he said... "I don't do scared!"

What? Seriously? – Nope – George's faith in the Lord was so strong and so amazing that I will never forget his answer!

That's my greatest memory of Carol's hospital stay... and guess what? Pastor George – you were right!

Patti Meredith

Chapter 3 – "Red Light"

Day 12 – (Day 5 @ Thomas Jefferson University Hospital)
Thursday, August 13, 2009

At 3:00 am Carol started moving her right index finger up and down in front of her eyes. That finger has a pulse-oximeter on it that emits a red light. As I watched this behavior I said, "Carol, can you see that?" She said "I think I can."

During the morning rounds, the doctors confirmed she could was seeing light again and she was starting to see shadows. They gave Carol a MRI in the morning. Carol began to be able to move her left hand. Dr. DeShant told us that there was evidence of minor stroking in Carol's occipital lobe that controls vision and that there will be resulting damage.

They also gave Carol an Angiogram at about 2:00 am Friday morning. Dr. Randazzo, who did the "Angio" said that Carol had what appeared to be vasculitis throughout her whole brain. Dr. Randazzo and the rest of the staff said that they had already been treating her with the medicine that would be prescribed for vasculitis since early in the week.

George

All I remember is the angiogram machine made a knock-knock-knocking sound as it performed its duty. And I was fairly sure it wasn't on heaven's door!

Carol

Day 13 – (Day 6 @ TJUH) Friday, August 14, 2009

Carol's vision is improving. She is starting to see faces and she can accurately tell how many fingers a doctor is holding up before her - if they are held a particular location. Carol can lift her arm off the bed to a height of about 15 inches. The doctors predict that Carol's vision will improve. Dr. Jabbour comes in and tells Carol that there were pin-points of infarction in her occipital lobe and he believed her vision would improve and possibly come back to her baseline vision. The medicine Carol's been receiving to elevate her BP was neo-synepherine. The rheumatologists presented a theory that maybe Carol was suffering from an auto-immune syndrome. They suggest that Carol be taken off neo-synepherine. They backed off the "neo" to see how Carol would respond. She quickly lost the strength in her left arm and at that point her right leg was becoming weaker. They quickly brought back the previous level of neo.

Carol's brother, Ronnie Rookstool, flew up from Florida to see his baby sister. Ronnie has been a lifelong seaman. A boat captain for most of his life, Ronnie now builds ocean-going yachts for the company he heads up, Sea Force Nine in Palmetto, Florida. Ronnie was staying tuned to the daily updates; but had to lay his eyes on his sister to get a sense for how she was doing. Ronnie was caring, concerned and worried about his "Lee-la". We had a good talk in the hallway in Jefferson and he enjoyed his time with Carol and offered any help he and his wife, Gail, could give. Carol enjoyed his visit and we appreciated Ronnie flying up to be with her.

Day 14 – (Day 7 @ TJUH) Saturday, August 15, 2009

Continuing Triple H therapy Carol's symptoms continue to improve. The left arm is almost up to where it was yesterday. Her vision is getting a little clearer.

George

Annabell Thorn, a sister-in-Christ and a friend of 36 years

Ooh eeh ooh ah aah
Ting tang
Walla walla bing bang

It wasn't fall yet, but Halloween decorations were in the stores already. When I saw the singing pumpkin, my only thought was that it might make Carol smile. So that's why I bought it.

I didn't understand what was going on with her, but it seemed serious. I asked my friend, Charlotte, to go with me to visit Carol in the hospital in Philadelphia. That's when I gave her the singing pumpkin.

When we walked in her room she was trying to be her usual gracious self, but it was difficult for her. They said, "Can you see Annabell?" and she said, "Yes, she's right here." But she really wasn't looking where I was. She showed us how she had to practice "carrying a pizza box" because she couldn't move her hands very well.

We hadn't been there too long when she turned to George and said, "It's been a long day." That's when we knew it was time to go and she was getting tired.

But, yes, the singing pumpkin did make her smile.

I remember the overwhelming feeling of sadness I felt whenever I would let my mind wander to the possibility that Carol might die. I couldn't imagine walking into Friendship Bible Church and her not being there. It would bring tears to my eyes and I would remind myself of God's sovereignty, His love, His promises to work things out for good, and His omniscient plan for all of us.

These are the verses I trust in when I pray for Carol and George:

> *"For My thoughts are not your thoughts,*
> *Nor are your ways My ways," declares the Lord.*
> *"For as the heavens are higher than the earth,*
> *So are My ways higher than your ways*
> *And My thoughts than your thoughts." (Isaiah 55:8-9)*

> *"For I know the plans that I have for you," declares the Lord, "plans for welfare and not for calamity to give you a future and a hope." (Jeremiah 29:11)*

> *And we know that God causes all things to work together for good to those who love God, to those who are called according to His purpose. (Romans 8:28)*

Annabell Thorn

Day 15 – (Day 8 @ TJUH) Sunday, August 16, 2009

Continuing Triple H therapy Carol's symptoms continue to improve. The left arm can be raised all the way up. Her vision is getting clearer. The neuro-docs are ruling out the vasculitis diagnosis because the blood tests for it all came back

25

negative. Their idea is it is either vasospasms or vasoconstriction.

George

As part of the daily rounds in the hospital, a team of physicians would visit my room, examine my chart, and quiz me concerning details of my mental and physical capacities. I became acutely appreciative of the Hippocratic Oath during these times; especially the "do no harm" clause. For over a week the staff of Jefferson had been taking extreme care of my every need and each day during morning rounds when asked where I was, I routinely answered, University of Pennsylvania! (One of Jefferson's close and capable competitors in the Philadelphia metropolitan area). And when asked what year it was, my daily reply was 1989! (A mere 20 years off! And the year my mother went home to Glory) Despite this, no member of the staff ever "did me any harm!"

Carol

A friend's recollection – Susan Hitzel (Roommate in college and lifelong friend)

Carol has been one of the biggest influences in my life. As far back as high school, she has always served as a role model for me. I have always admired her intelligence, humor, strength, beauty, and loyalty. She has the habit of enriching the lives of those she befriends. She makes each person feel as if he or she is a valuable and special human being.

When I received the news that she had suffered some sort of seizure/stroke event, I went with her sister to the hospital to see her. I cannot find the words to describe my feelings when I saw her! She was barely able to see or speak. I saw very little evidence of the personality I had adored for decades. The look of fear and confusion in her eyes made me physically sick. I prayed and prayed that God would give her back to us.

I couldn't imagine a world without her, all of her! So I didn't. I just assumed she would return. And each time I saw her, she did return little by little. I kept praying and waiting, and then waiting, and then it happened! Her humor returned. That's when I knew she would be alright! She has worked harder than most of us can even imagine recovering from this brain injury. I thank the Lord for giving her back to us, and for George, who has loved and supported her all along. They are a rare and wonderful couple who have been an inspiration to us all.

Susan (Herb) Hitzel

Day 16 – (Day 9 @ TJUH) Monday, August 17, 2009

Carol is transferred from the Neuroscience Building on the neurosurgery floor to another Neurological ICU at the main Thomas Jefferson building – the Gibbon Building on 10th between Sansom & Chestnut streets in Philadelphia. It was about a two block ride in an ambulance.

Carol is still under Neurology but she is no longer a possible candidate for Brain Surgery so she was moved to Gibbon.

Day 17 – (Day 10 @ TJUH) Tuesday, August 18, 2009

Vision - still improving - she can see and count fingers that are flashed in many positions in front of her. There are some regions where she can't see

27

them. She can see faces generally, but she is still having huge depth perception problems.

Motor Abilities - legs are strong with wiggling toes. Her right arm and hand are fine. Her left arm requires a lot of concentration to move, but after it starts, she can lift it over her head. She was able today to voluntarily move the fingers on her left hand - a first since last Wednesday. We are hoping for a thumb's up on her left hand at some point.

Cognitive Abilities - Process thoughts are scrambled. Anything that has a beginning, middle and end Carol is having trouble putting together. Her short-term memory is weak but getting stronger. I think after a week of "Neuro" nurses and doctors asking her, she is finally absorbing that it is 2009.

Spirits - Her spirits are great. She has been singing hymns, when she gets a little scared. She has been brave and determined. Everywhere she goes she is becoming a favorite!

Diagnosis – This has been a mystery. The "White Coats" have been telling me the same thing every day. The entire Neuroscience ICU staff meets daily to discuss every patient, and Carol's case is still too difficult to diagnose. The best guess from the Neurology and Rheumatology staffs is Reversible Cerebral Vasoconstriction Syndrome. This syndrome, I understand, was first isolated in 1988 by two researchers by the names of Gregory Call and Marie Fleming. Further study has yielded the following understanding.

28

Reversible cerebral vasoconstriction syndrome (RCVS, sometimes called Call-Fleming syndrome) is a disease characterized by a weeks-long course of thunderclap headaches, sometimes focal neurologic signs, and occasionally seizures. Symptoms are thought to arise from transient abnormalities in the blood vessels of the brain... For the vast majority of patients, all symptoms disappear on their own within three weeks. Deficits persist in a small minority of patients, with severe complications or death being very rare. Because symptoms resemble a variety of life-threatening conditions, differential diagnosis is necessary. (**Mehdi, A. & Hajj-Ali, R. A**. (2014). "Reversible cerebral vasoconstriction syndrome: a comprehensive update." Current Pain and Headache Reports.)

As one doctor told me, the best thing about this diagnosis is the word "reversible." If this diagnosis is correct, RCVS has to run its course which can be as long as several weeks. Carol will need rehab and should be starting soon. The second theory is vasospasms which usually run their course in 21 days.

For either diagnosis, the treatment has included a Triple H therapy. One of the three H's is "hypertension" where Carol's blood pressure is being held at a slightly higher than normal state to allow blood to continue to pass through her compromised brain vessels and profuse to all areas of her brain. That is making it possible for her to get stronger as her vessel problems straighten out.

Day 18 – (Day 11 @ TJUH) Wednesday, August 19, 2009

Carol's vision is still improving. She is seeing colors fairly well.

Motor Abilities - She is able to move her left arm with less concentration and can lift it over her head easily. Also, she is able to spread out her fingers on her left hand - that's a first. We are hoping for a thumb's up on her left hand at some point.

Cognitive Abilities – No change

Spirits - Her spirits are great. She is enjoying seeing visitors. She has a very squeezable stuffed teddy bear that she likes holding.

George

Whoever gave me this bear, thank you so much!

One of the things that has been a constant in my life is my long hair. For those of you who know me, you know how I feel about change. I have had the same hairstyle for my entire life! At first, it was because my mother liked long hair. In my teens and twenties, it was because I liked long hair. In my thirties, it was because I realized I did not know how to take care of a styled haircut. In my 40s and 50s it was because my husband liked long hair. In my sixties it just is! Debbie Holliday, my dearest friend, has, shall we say, "strongly encouraged" me to cut my hair for many years. Other friends have sent me magazine clippings of haircuts they thought would look good on me; to no avail. In fact, my hair is the same length it was in my high school graduation pictures! At this point in my stay in Jefferson, a Cranial Angiogram was prescribed. If anyone has had a cranial angiogram, you can identify with what I am about to say. The process starts with your head being covered with glue for the electrodes, lots and lots of glue! The purpose of the glue is to hold a multitude of tiny electrodes in place on your head. You are then placed in a body length tube. I was, of course, in my new normal state of oblivion, but still remember the knocking sounds as the tube rotated for what seemed like hours. Fast forward to Day 11 of my stay at Jefferson... imagine what my head looked like and what my hair looked and felt like after having had this procedure! It felt to me like the artificial piles of poop people used to put out on the sidewalks on April Fool's Day. Sticky was not the word!

Enter, my dearest friend Debbie, the same Debbie who had encouraged me to cut my hair for years. She sat for hours and hours in my hospital room and piece by piece painstakingly combed out almost every bit of that glue from my matted head. Debbie is a friend, a sister in Christ, and to this day, a proponent of short hair on sixty-something year olds! The Bible tells us, "There is a friend who sticks (no pun intended!) closer than a brother." Debbie is that kind of friend. I pray that I am that kind of friend to her. I also pray you have that kind of friend in your life.

Carol

Teresa Littley, a dear friend since my freshman year of high school

I first learned of Rook's illness while trying to set up a dinner date for Rook, our friend, Bettie and me. Bettie and I had both been e-mailing her and not getting a response. So I called Carol's office at Stockton, no answer. Then I called the main number and got someone

(I think it was probably Carol's friend, Roseann) who I could tell recognized my name but did not identify herself – "Carol's not in". "OK," I said... I will try her at home... "she's not home either" in a tone of voice that was just not sounding right. I called the house and thankfully got Evie (Carol's sister) on the phone. I am thinking to myself this can't be good – little did I know.

Evie gave me the rundown – sick in Colorado – made it home – then Sunday morning urgent care to the Mainland Regional ER – then to Jefferson Neuro – she was calm – pragmatic. Since I was at work I then e-mailed Bettie and Susan (another high school friend) – to let them know something was seriously wrong. A day or two later I realized I did not have a phone number for our mutual friend, Donald, so I wrote him a note to let him know as well. He called me the day he got the note.

I tried to get George on the phone but couldn't reach him – so we went a couple of days not sure what was what – probably spoke to Evie again during that time - she had told me George said "No Visitors Allowed" – a source of contention here at home – my son, Zack, kept saying, "I can't believe you – these people have been there for you for every crisis and you are not going – what is your problem?" I said I need to respect their wishes and wait till I can at least talk to George.

On the Friday night of that week, Bettie and her husband, Chuck, and I went out to Oyster Creek, a restaurant in our area. We were all concerned and upset – while we were out, Zack got a call from George who wanted to call my cell – people who know me know how well that works. Luckily, we finally spoke live when I got home. He asked me to pass the word on to others.

There is no more helpless feeling than not being able to help someone you love when they are in pain – so frustrating... you just want to do something – anything.

We got the OK to visit – so on August 18th, Evie and I went to Thomas Jefferson Hospital – it turned out we arrived during a move to another room – the ICU room they keep ready for the President of the United States when he comes to Philadelphia – "pretty cool" I remember thinking. Zack had made brownies for me to take for the staff – when Rook heard that she said, "That's my job!"

As I remember Evie had visited once before and warned me it would be tough – it was.

Rook had lost her vision in the time before the visit but was regaining it – she recognized me! George looked happy to see us, weary and overwhelmed – "I'm fine, I'm fine" no George – you were not fine somehow you were hanging on with all you had. I think we stayed less than an hour – I remember thinking this is a LONG, LONG road back IF it is a road that could ever be traveled.

Once George got the email updates set up it was so great to be able to know every day what was happening. I hope it helped him as much as it helped his friends! I think it was a week or so later Bettie and I visited at Jeff – I saw a big improvement in Rook and a more exhausted George who was still "fine!" as in why are you asking about me... don't ask! I remember bringing along a children's Golden Book because Rook was trying to relearn how to read – it was a Christmas book.

It was shortly after that we got the good news about the move to the Betty Bacharach Rehabilitation Hospital near home. I remember being shocked how much better Rook looked when I visited her there – then we heard that Ashley, her golden retriever, had visited and knew that could only have been a great day! Some of the Rookstool orneriness showed up at BBRH – another good sign!

I think in some ways the ongoing convalescence at home was hardest on both of you. In these situations – the obvious crisis passes – school starts – people get back to their regular routines – but your lives are never the same. It is a gigantic challenge!

I hope I was a help then on same level; I honestly can't remember. I do know that around Thanksgiving and Christmas there was much frustration because Rook could not make her traditional dishes and desserts – couldn't set the table, etc. because of ongoing issues. I know she hated to be driven everywhere and that the smallest tasks were monumental undertakings, often leading to tears.

The relentlessness of all this had to take a toll on George, but he would never admit it to anyone.

Rook – in the years since it has been amazing how far you have come. Back to work, traveling and listening to your old friend's mini-dramas. When George was sick in 2010, you held it together. Even this last six months you seem more and more like your old pre-summer 2009 self! I think being retired and the prospect of it has been better for you than you may have realized it would be. Your marriage is an inspiration – talk about "in sickness and in health"! I think the very best thing is your outlook on the things you just can't do or do well any more –

accepting and grateful for the things you can do – that is a really hard lesson and some days I know it is really tough but you keep moving on and it's great to see!

Teresa Littley

Diagnosis - The leading theory is still Reversible Cerebral Vasoconstriction Syndrome. That's good, the diagnosis de jour we were having was becoming nerve-wracking. The treatment is steroids and Triple H therapy. Triple H therapy includes "hypertension" where Carol's blood pressure is being held slightly higher than normal to allow blood to continue to pass through her compromised brain vessels and profuse to all areas of her brain - that is making it possible for her to get stronger as her vessel problems straighten out. RCVS has to run its course which can take several weeks. A social worker spoke to me yesterday about therapy which can start soon either in Philadelphia or somewhere in South Jersey.

George

Marieann Bannon – a good friend from church and a co-worker at Stockton

Here's my recollection of everything as close to the order it happened to the best of my ability.

First, I remember hearing about the incident at church on the Sunday night after it happened. We said a prayer for Carol and everyone around her, friends who were on vacation with them, and the doctors.

35

I remember too, that Carol was in Jefferson Neuroscience Hospital in Philadelphia. She still couldn't see well and had those things on her legs to help make the blood circulate due to her not getting out of bed. I did go visit and brought a stuffed dog to keep Carol company in the hospital. I remember hearing that Carol would be singing hymns while in the hospital and there were many prayers said. I also heard there were several people visiting Carol while at Jefferson.

Eventually Carol's vision improved, but she had a hard time being able to drive right away. Our friend, Roseann Stollenwerk, helped a lot with that. There were a lot of people who tried to help where they could, cooking and cleaning the house so George could stay with Carol.

Marieann Bannan

Chapter 4 - "Pizza Boxes"

As anyone knows who has spent any time in a hospital, along with the wonderful staff, routine is a key ingredient to recovery. Once I had finally conquered the name of the hospital that was caring for me and the year in which I was living we then moved on to somewhat more complex concepts, such as could I hold an imaginary pizza box up with both hands. ("baby steps") Now each morning my doctors checked my vitals and instead of quizzing me about my location and calendar concepts, they asked me to raise both hands above my head in unison and hold them there as if I were holding an imaginary pizza box. If you have not already lost interest in my daily progress as so graciously supplied by my husband, you realize my left arm is not working well. Add to this a number of intravenous attachments and a more than usual diminished mental capacity. So, holding this pizza box was truly a monumental task. I would feebly attempt it daily and secretly practice it nightly in order to clear this hurdle and move closer to being released from Jefferson! Each night when George visited, he said "pizza box" at various times during his stay. Eventually, my left arm caught up to my right. To this day, I cannot look at a pizza box as most people do.

Carol

Day 19 – (Day 12 @ TJUH) Thursday, August 20, 2009

Vision - still improving - Carol read the date from the marker board on the wall next to her bed yesterday. She could read the word "August" which suggests that she should be able to read better as her eyes and brain get better.

37

Motor Abilities - Her left arm and hand continue to get stronger. She is able to spread out her fingers. We are still hoping for a "thumbs up" on her left hand soon.

Cognitive Abilities - Process thoughts are still scrambled. Her short-term memory is getting better. She knows the month and year and she knows where she is.

Spirits - Her spirits are great. She is enjoying seeing visitors. Her attitude is wonderful. The day we got married, Carol moved from her mom's house to our first home, so Carol has never had to sleep by herself. Since she has been moved to the Gibbon Building, the staff has chased me out of the room at the end of visiting hours. Sleeping alone in a hospital room with its beeps and sounds has been a little scary for Carol... but each night she gets a little better with it. She holds the call button control in her right hand and knows the nurse will come if she needs something.

Diagnosis – No change

The Thomas Jefferson "neuro" team is doing Dopplers of Carol's brain each day to check the level of constriction. The attending doctor is Dr. Rodney Bell and he says that Carol's brain vessels are returning to the normal range for blood velocity...which means the narrowing is subsiding. Soon they will try to wean Carol off her neosynepherine to see if she can function properly without the intravenous medication that is raising her blood pressure. When she is off this medicine, she may be on her way to rehab.

Yesterday, a woman named Diana from Betty Bacharach Institute for Rehabilitation interviewed Carol and went through her charts - it looks like Carol might be coming to Bacharach in Galloway Township for rehab. It will be nice to have her so close to home. What's great about Bacharach is it is connected to the Atlanticare Regional Medical Center so if Carol needs any medical attention they will just have to wheel her down the hall to the hospital.

Beginning on August 20, I started writing a devotional idea each day entitled "Morning Thoughts" which I sent out to the extensive list of people who had been praying for Carol. There were a few skips, but these thoughts run through to the last entry on September 16. We will add these ideas into the running narrative on the day they were written. They show our spiritual thoughts during this time.

Morning Thoughts - August 20, 2009

As I seek strength each day to do what I have to for Carol, I have been doing a lot of thinking with praying. I'm led to pass some of those thoughts on to you. If they seem to be the ramblings of a distraught husband, well consider it to be therapy for me to get it out…and maybe pray for my sleep-deprived soul.

The Word says that "We know that God causes all things to work together for good to those who love God, to those called according to His purpose." (Romans 8:28) Carol certainly loves God and is called to His purpose so we can stand on this promise from God Himself. God created our bodies and our eyes to respond to the light He spoke into existence. His knowledge and ability totally eclipse the capacities of the greatest neurosurgeons. So the surgeons and neurologists work and we continue to come to the throne of grace and ask for His help.

Photons, packets of light energy, traveling millions of miles through space to enter our atmosphere to light and heat the earth is His idea. How those light beams strike and reflect off objects and are captured by our eyes creating a neural impulse traveling from the retina through the optic nerve to the vision centers in the occipital region of the brain is His design. He has the patent on that process. And how neurons locked in that sealed gray mass fire and present to our minds the phenomenon of vision is undeniably supernatural. So we come to the One who loves Carol and made her and ask for help.

I am convinced God has a good purpose in all this - and that might not include Carol regaining all of her sight, that is totally up to an all-wise and loving God. I am comforted by the invitation presented by the writer of Hebrews…

> *"Let us therefore come boldly unto the throne of grace, that we may obtain mercy, and find grace to help in time of need." Hebrews 4:16*

*(Resource – **More Than Meets the Eye**, Richard Swenson, Navpress, Colorado Springs 2000)*

*The book I cite here, **More Than Meets the Eye, Fascinating Glimpses of God's Power and Design**, is a book I turned to often during this time. This work was always a favorite of mine, but became especially near to me during this time. Dr. Swenson has the unique resume of being a medical doctor who had an undergraduate degree in physics and was a believer in Jesus Christ. It was a perfect combination for me, a physics teacher and pastor, who had a beloved wife going through a medically traumatic episode. His book is such a comfort to me. I borrowed extensively during our harrowing autumn of 2009 to gain perspective. I want to thank Richard for his help by making his thoughts available to his readers. The Bible is accurate when it states as "Iron sharpens iron, so one man sharpens another." (Prov.27:17)*

Day 20 – (Day 13 @ TJUH) Friday, August 21, 2009

Vision continues to get better.

Motor Abilities – No "thumbs up" yet with Carol's left hand, but everything else seems to be working better.

Cognitive Abilities – No change

Spirits are still good.

Diagnosis – No change.

George

Anyone who is reading this and knows me, knows my love of coffee. Over the years I have drunk and still drink too much of it and enjoy every drop. I was unable to feed myself in the hospital and am eternally grateful to those who fed me daily. It was routinely a young woman who, I am certain, had a number of patients to care for, most of whom were in situations similar to mine. One morning I was being fed breakfast and when it came time for my sip of coffee, the young lady asked if I would like to hold the cup and drink it myself. That sounded good to me! Being unaware of the level of my visual acuity, or lack thereof, I didn't realize that locating the table on which the cup rested would be, for me, tantamount to landing the lunar module on the moon! So, there I sat, cup in hand, for what seemed to be an eternity. Unable to locate the table and concentrating so intently on so doing, the coffee became cold and my arm became very tired! My breakfast angel did return and we decided I was not yet ready to drink on my own! Don't ever take the smallest detail of your life for granted. I know I don't each time I take a sip of hot coffee.

Carol

Morning Thoughts - August 21, 2009

The Bible teaches that we should only worship God. Indeed, it's the first commandment… "Thou shalt have no other gods before Me." (Exodus 20:3) There is no one else to worship. There is no thing to worship. In Ephesians 3:20, the Word says "Now to Him who is able to do exceeding abundantly beyond all that we ask or think, according to the power that works within us, to Him be the glory in the church and in Christ Jesus to all generations forever and ever. Amen."

When Carol and I were in Colorado before one of our meals a young ranch hand named Chris was asked to pray. In his prayer, surrounded by the Rocky Mountains, he prayed, "God help us not to be so impressed with the beauty of the creation around us that we forget to praise the Creator who made it all."

When we are in our right minds we are able to distinguish the created things around us from the Creator. Our sane worship has to be directed to the One who made everything and not on the things He made. The beauty and wisdom of what we see around us speak of an overwhelming intelligence and creativity.

Now in Carol's case, we must not worship and serve the healing, we must worship and love the One who can heal. If we worship the healing, then really our prayers are some kind of con game where we only pray because we want something and when we get it we walk away with no more time for God nor thought of Him. If our children acted like that we would want to smack them.

Now, our relationship with our heavenly Father through Jesus is more important than any created thing including Carol's healing. When we are short-sighted we pray and pray and pray and if God doesn't heal we go away angry and disappointed because God didn't give us what we wanted. Our tantrum doesn't change the fact that He is God and He is the only One to Whom we can turn. He heals when He sovereignly desires to for His purpose.

Carol's illness has the potential to draw us close or even to establish a relationship with the God Carol worships and loves. God's greater plan is to draw men and women to the Savior who loved us and died for our sins so we can fellowship with Him and be able to know and worship Him.

Day 21 – (Day 14 @ TJUH) Saturday, August 22, 2009

Vision - still improving – Carol's eyes are tracking better. She is doing a better job of looking directly at the person who is talking to her. The neurologists were in to see Carol for an exam. One of them said Carol appears to have Balint's Syndrome. Balint's is a neurological disorder where a patient has a lack of coordination of hand and eye movements, an inability to voluntarily guide eye movements and an inability to perceive more than one object at a time.

Motor Abilities - Her left arm and hand continue to get stronger. A neurologist is starting to help Carol write again. When Carol started to regain the ability to write, she wrote one letter on top of another letter. So, she needed to relearn the idea of moving across the page as she prints successive letters.

44

Cognitive Abilities - Short Term Memory continues to improve.

Spirits - Her spirits are very good. She is determined to get better with God's help.

One of the neurologists said the latest charting of Carol's constrictions shows the left side of her brain is down to a very low level of constriction, essentially back to normal. The doctor said her right side is at a medium level of constriction... that side's vessel function has to get down to where the left side is for her to really get back to normal. When it does, Carol will be on her way to Bacharach for rehab. Very good news!

Morning Thoughts - August 22, 2009

Carol's old friend Andy Bush, who now lives in Phoenix, sent Carol a card in which she wrote and said she was praying for her. Andy is Jewish, so she said "Jewish prayers are like Christian prayers only louder."

Carol appreciates all the prayers whether they are soft or loud. Carol loves sending cards. She has driven me nuts for 25 years with all the cards she sends. I told her once that she sends more Mother's Day cards than others send Christmas cards. But it always brings joy to her heart to send some expression of concern, love or encouragement. Many of you have received multiple missives of kindness from Carol.

Carol appreciates all the cards she has received since she has been in Jefferson. I sit next to her bed and read them all to her. So keep them coming! You can send them to Carol by just mailing them to me. I'll bring them up and add them to the stack.

All those cards, mounting up in her room, are a harvest of all the acts of kindness Carol has shown to others over the years. It's like a mountain of testimony of how she has reached out to so many when they needed to be encouraged, congratulated, or just loved. There's a poem that is apt…

> *I have wept in the night*
> *For the shortness of sight,*
> *That to somebody's need made me blind:*
> *But I never have yet*

Felt a twinge of regret,
For being a little too kind.

- *Anonymous*

Day 22 – (Day 15 @ TJUH) Sunday, August 23, 2009

Vision - still improving - Carol is actually doing OK on voluntary eye movements and the ability to perceive more than one object... currently she has great difficulty with eye-hand coordination. We'll keep praying.

Motor and cognitive abilities are about the same.

Spirits - Her spirits are very good. She is determined to get better with God's help. Tomorrow is Carol's birthday - she is getting fried chicken from Wash's Inn in Pleasantville, New Jersey. She's going to love that.

Diagnosis - The diagnosis is still Reversible Vaso-Constriction Syndrome. The treatment is steroids and Triple H therapy.

Carol gets Dopplers of her brain twice a day... they are showing a continued decrease in vessel constriction. If this trend continues, they will start to wean her off the neosynepherine. Once she's off that medicine, she will be able to get out of bed and start walking again.

George

John Quinn, George's twin brother, is the executive pastor of the Friendship Bible Church and an

associate professor of mathematics education at Stockton University. John and wonderful wife, Carol, wrote this piece on their delivery of Carol's favorite meal.

Wash's Chicken

We were all praying for Carol's recovery. Her birthday was approaching. What could help Rook find new healing? Ahhh … a bit of inspiration! Fried chicken! Carol's custom was to carefully watch her diet throughout the whole year. However, on her birthday ... on that special day, she would indulge in some fried chicken. Not just any-old fried chicken, her delight was the deep-fried, mouth-watering delicacy that could only be secured from Wash's Inn. Wash's Inn? This was an urban tavern that was famous for tasty, succulent chicken - cooked to golden perfection, and seasoned exquisitely. Could these prized morsels have the key to Carol's recovery? It was worth a shot. We called ahead. John went in to Wash's. Carol stayed in the car … with it running! The chicken was secured and now for the critical trip from Pleasantville to Philadelphia.

We arrived. Although Carol's vision was still on the mend, nothing was wrong with her olfactory nerve. The aroma of Wash's chicken announced our arrival. Sweet savor filled the air. We prayed for healing and then forgiveness! Carol, and the rest of us, dug into this poultry treasure. Convinced of God's healing power and the goodness of Wash's chicken, we watched to see if this could be the secret to recovery. As the days and weeks passed by, Carol's recovery was wonderful to see. However, we know that there was a critical pivot in her story.

Wash's Inn is no longer in business today. But alas, it spectacularly served its purpose while on earth. The

48

healing balm of its savory juices will always be an
essential part of Rook's story.

EUREKA! The day did finally arrive when the
processional of doctors entered my room, checked my
vitals and I, yes I, raised BOTH arms above my head and
held that all too elusive pizza box! I am sure it was my
imagination, but somewhere in the background of that
hospital room I could have sworn I heard the theme from
Chariots of Fire.

Carol

Chapter 5 – "Worship Songs"

On February 10, 2004, George called me on the way home from work and told me he thought he was having a heart attack. He was. The Lord in His infinite mercy spared him and we have been thankful and grateful each day since. If you have been hospitalized for any length of time, you are familiar with the breathing tube! Breathe into the mouthpiece and attempt to hold a little ball up in the air. When George was released from the hospital, part of his therapy was to practice utilizing his lungs. Since we did not have a breathing tube, we sang hymns as an exercise to increase his lung capacity. Well now it was my turn to experience the healing power of music. Our worship leader at that time, a gifted young man named Scott Aspenberg, recorded a CD of worship songs for me. A co-worker, Joanna Frankel, a concert harpist, recorded a CD of her playing. George brought a CD player and the CDs to my room. Each night right before he left, he would put it on. As he already wrote, I had never slept alone prior to this hospitalization. The music and words brought such comfort to me in his absence! I can't help but remember the words to the hymn, "Redeemed" by Fanny Crosby:

> I know I shall see in His Beauty
> The King in whose law I delight;
> Who lovingly gardeth my footsteps,
> And giveth me songs in the night.

Through these gifted musicians, as always, the Lord kept His promise! Not only were these songs a solace to me, but several of my caregivers expressed how much they appreciated the sweet sounds that emanated from my room through the nights.

Day 23 – (Day 16 @ TJUH) Monday, August 24, 2009

Carol is in the Thomas Jefferson Gibbon Building (Room 9320) on 10th between Sansom and Chestnut. It is the main Jefferson building with the atrium. If you want to visit - the hours are 12 Noon to 8:30 PM.

Vision - the doctors are hopeful that Carol's vision will continue to improve. We'll keep praying.

Motor Abilities - Her left arm and hand continue to get stronger. We're bringing Carol a tennis ball to squeeze to strengthen that hand and arm. A neurologist is starting to help Carol write again.

Cognitive Abilities - Short Term Memory continues to improve. Her brain function seems to be getting better & better. She's listening every night to a CD of Praise Songs from Scott and the harp music from Joanna. The music has seemed to calm her down and is allowing her to sleep better.

Spirits – Her spirits are very good. Today's Carol's birthday – my twin brother John and his wife Carol and their children, Danielle and George, brought fried chicken from Wash's Inn in Pleasantville to Carol. She loved every morsel. We had birthday cake in the room and sang "Happy Birthday" to her.

George

You may recall I wrote of my love for coffee earlier. I do love coffee, but fried chicken was and is my favorite repasts! And while any fried chicken will do, the fried chicken produced by Wash's Inn was to die for! John and Carol knew my proclivity for it and were kind enough to transport it some sixty miles west to Jefferson for me for

51

my first, and hopefully, last birthday celebration in the hospital. While I do have major gaps in my memory, this fried chicken I distinctly remember! It was delicious and to this day, John attributes my recovery from this point on to my ingestion of it! On a somewhat more philosophical note, Wash's is no longer in business. However, the love of family and friends expressed in so many ways during my time of affliction as well as the sovereignty of my Savior will never pass away.

Carol

The new neurologist said the CT Scan she had yesterday shows that amazingly (to them) there was not nearly as much damage to the brain as they originally thought. Areas they thought were damaged seemed to have blood flow and were coming back. Good news!

Thanks for all your prayers gestures of kindness - please keep approaching the throne of grace for Carol.

George

Morning Thoughts – August 24, 2009

And they came to Bethsaida. And they brought a blind man to Him, and entreated Him to touch him. And taking the blind man by the hand, He brought him out of the village; and after spitting on his eyes, and laying His hands upon him, He asked him, "Do you see anything?" And He looked up and said, "I see men, for I am seeing them like trees, walking about." Then again He laid His hands upon his eyes; and looked intently and was restored, and began to see clearly. (Mk.9:22-25)

This is a fascinating account of Jesus' healing a blind man. The miracle apparently took place in stages. After spitting on his eyes and laying His hand on him, the man began to see but men looked like moving trees. He laid His hands upon his eyes again and then the man's vision was completely restored.

Could it be that the vision Carol has regained is like her seeing men like trees, and the Lord must touch her eyes again to completely restore her sight? The neurologists would say that's impossible – once neurons are destroyed they can never recover. I know God has no problem with doing what we consider impossible. In this story there was no hope for the blind man until Jesus touched him. For Carol, it is clear, it has to be His hand that needs to touch her eyes.

Day 24 – (Day 17 @ TJUH) Tuesday, August 25, 2009

Vision - We are going to try to read today.

Motor Abilities - Her left arm and hand continue to get stronger. Carol's friend Roseann, who works with her, brought home a stress relief ball from Stockton for Carol to squeeze to strengthen her hand and arm.

Spirits - Her spirits are very good. Carol's birthday went well - she really enjoyed the fried chicken from Wash's in Pleasantville. She is also getting her sense of humor back... look out!

Diagnosis - Her anti-spasm med is nimodipine and that tends to drop her blood pressure, so the Neo has to be stepped up to keep the BP higher. They have decreased the nimodipine from 6 times a day to 4 times a day... so that will decrease the need for additional neosynepherine.

Carol gets Dopplers of her brain twice a day... they are now showing a continued decrease in vessel constriction now on both sides.

Thanks for all your prayers and gestures of kindness - please keep approaching the throne of grace.

Morning Thoughts – August 25, 2009

The Word says…

> *And Jesus passed on from there, two blind men followed Him, crying out, and saying, "Have mercy on us, Son of David!" And after He had come into the house, the blind men came up to Him and Jesus said to them, "Do you believe that I am able to do this?" They said to Him, "Yes, Lord." Then He touched their eyes, saying, "Be it done to you according to your faith." And their eyes were opened. (Mt.9:27-30a)*

Healing the blind was part of our Lord's ministry. Every person who knows the Lord Jesus and believes the Word of God agrees on at least two basic truths:

1. *God is God and He can heal. He built our bodies and He can heal them. There's no question in anyone's mind who reads and believes his or her Bible that Almighty God, who created us and redeemed us through the Lord Jesus Christ, can heal us.*

2. *God does heal, at times and in situations where it pleases Him. It's evident that God doesn't always heal. We all will die. These physical bodies are mortal… meaning they are facing a death event. But God can and does heal when it is in His perfect will and often in response to our faith.*

When these blind men cried out to Jesus, "Have mercy on us, Son of David!", He asked, before restoring their sight, "Do you believe that I am able to do this?" Can we believe that the Lord Jesus can do anything we need Him to do for us today?

We cannot heal anyone, but we can follow the blind men's example. We can believe. As I see it, we certainly have the easy job. We believe. God heals. That works!

Day 25 – (Day 18 @ TJUH) Wednesday, August 26, 2009

Vision - We started reading. We started with a children's reader. Carol's mental ability is still post-graduate, but she needs to connect again seeing words and reading them.

Cognitive Abilities - Short Term Memory continues to improve. Her brain function seems to be getting better and better. Our friend, Pastor Farmer, added a Gaither's Band CD to Carol's night listening selections. The music seems to calm her and allows her to sleep better.

Carol's Dopplers are showing no vessel constriction now on both sides.

Thanks for all your prayers and gestures of kindness - please keep approaching the throne of grace.

Day 26 – (Day 19 @ TJUH) Thursday, August 27, 2009

Vision - We read from a child's reader for a second day.

Cognitive Abilities - Short Term Memory is getting stronger. She is trying to force herself to

56

remember recent events and even the routes she takes to get to work.

Spirits - Very good.

Carol is officially finished with the Dopplers of her brain twice a day... "The Whitecoats" believe there is no sign of vessel constriction on either side. Thank you Lord!

Morning Thoughts – August 27, 2009

Dr. Michael Moussouttas, Carol's Attending Neurologist a couple of days ago came to see Carol to ask her if she minded being famous. He said because Carol's case and symptomology is so unusual they want to write it up for a neurology journal. Carol, as you may know, works at Stockton University – her job is helping special needs students get whatever assistance they require to remain in college. Carol's response was if her case could help someone else with his or her illness, she would be happy to have them write it up and publish it.

The literature tells us that 50% of the individuals, who have a Sub Arachnoid Hemorrhage, as Carol did, die. So the fact that Carol is alive is a blessing. We know God is still on the throne and He is not finished with her.

I know God loves Carol. She loves Him too. The Word says… "Let your speech always be with grace, as though seasoned with salt, so that you will know how to respond to each person" (Colossians 4:6). Carol's response to Dr. Moussouttas was full of grace. The grace of… if my affliction could help someone else, use it.

We learn grace from God. His grace saves sinners. In a world full of them, it is our only means of rescue. God loved us so much that He sent Jesus to be our sin-bearer. He took our place in judgment that God's justice

58

*would be satisfied and as many as put their
trust in Him for salvation would receive His
forgiveness. It is a simple story…God's
Riches At Christ's Expense. Romans 10:9
says –*

*"If you confess with your mouth Jesus
as Lord, and believe in your heart that
God raised Him from the dead, you
will be saved" (Romans 10:9).*
*God made it simple enough that a child
could understand it, and yet we want it to be
more complicated. That is nothing more
than evidence of our fallen nature. We want
to do it ourselves. If that were possible then
Jesus did not have to come and die in our
place. Did He? If you have never
experienced the new birth that God can
give, pray to receive Jesus as your Savior
today. God's grace is amazing!*

Day 27 – (Day 20 @ TJUH) Friday, August 28, 2009

Vision - We read from a children's reader for a third
day.

Motor Abilities - The Occupational Therapist met
with Carol today. She gave Carol a series of
exercises to do visually and with her hands and
arms.

Diagnosis - The diagnosis is still Reversible
Cerebral Vasoconstriction Syndrome. The
treatment is steroids and Triple H therapy. Her
anti-spasm med is nimodipine and that tends to
drop her BP, so the Neo has to be stepped up to
keep the BP higher. They have decreased the

nimodipine from 6 times a day on Tuesday to 4 times a day Wednesday to 3 times a day Thursday to 2 times today, tomorrow zero... so that will decrease the need for additional neosynepherine. BP is looking good, no adverse signs.

No sign of vessel constriction on either side - Thank you Lord!

Thanks for all your prayers & gestures of kindness - please keep approaching the throne of grace for

Morning Thoughts - August 28, 2009

The Bible says His mercies are new every morning. (Lamentations 3:23) That's something for which to be thankful. We need the eyes of faith to see those mercies. Jeremiah, the prophet-author of Lamentations also makes the proclamation in that verse, "Great is Thy faithfulness."

When we add up events in our lives do we see His mercies and recognize His faithfulness? Paul writes,

> *"In everything give thanks for this is the will of God for you in Christ Jesus." (I Thessalonians 5:18)*

He tells us "In everything give thanks." Is this just poetic flourish? ...Some kind of spiritual hyperbole? Or did Paul actually mean IN EVERYTHING? I believe Paul, inspired by the Holy Spirit, meant literally what he wrote. It is the will of God to be thankful in everything!

If I get a broken leg, am I to shout for joy, "Hooray, look what happened to me!"? No, I can't rejoice for the pain, the inconvenience, or the disruption of my plans and the plans of others. But I can honestly and sincerely praise God because I know He means this very circumstance to bring blessing into my life and the lives of others.

We don't thank God in everything because God has a big need to hear our thanks. We thank God because our perspective needs to be God is almighty and purposeful and everything He allows in my life He allows for my blessing and His glory.

So the person of faith looks in every circumstance, no matter how dark and hard the details are, for the hand of God reaching down to bless.

In the process of yielding to His sovereign will with thanksgiving we will notice that God transforms our hearts with a lovely spirit to one of strength and health.

We have seen God's hand blessing through Carol's affliction. God's mercy and His faithfulness is, day by day, on display. For that we continue to be thankful!

Day 28 – (Day 21 @ TJUH) Saturday, August 29, 2009

Vision - still improving. We read from a children's reader for a fourth day.

Spirits – Carol's spirits are very good.

Thanks for all your prayers & gestures of kindness - please keep approaching the throne of grace.

Morning Thoughts - August 29, 2009

In our bodies is a three-pound brain which, as far as we know, is the most complex and orderly arrangement of matter in the universe. That thought alone requires a good bit of reflection and thanksgiving.

The brain, the pride and joy of the nervous system, is staggering in its abilities and complexity. Despite all our modern scientific research, we are only beginning to penetrate the brain's secrets.

The basic cell of the brain is called the "neuron". There are over 10 billion of them in each brain. All the information to form that huge number of individualized neurons was contained in the single microscopic fertilized egg we once were in our mother's womb. All the blueprints for every neuron and the body's plan to build itself including that three-pound brain was contained in that single tiny cell. It is truly breathtaking when we think about it. From freshman biology, we learn each neuron has an axon end and a branchlike dendrite end. Each neuron is in contact with thousands of other neurons, for a total of 100 trillion neurological interconnections.

Dr. Richard Swenson tells us, "If you were to stretch out all the neurons and dendritic connections in the brain and lay them end to end, they would reach a distance of 100 thousand miles. That distance is equal to circling the earth four times. The brain holds 10^{14} bits of information which is about a thousand times greater than the memory of the world's largest supercomputer.
While our supercomputers are tasked with such

mundane projects as determining the results of smashing subatomic particles together or calculating our national debt and who we owe the money to, the brain is successfully determining everything from life and death chemical reaction rates to synaptically firing the elements that make up our personalities."

The capacity of the brain is such that it can hold information equivalent to that contained in 25 million books, enough to fill a bookshelf 500 miles long. In contrast, the Library of Congress has 17 million volumes. That capacity is only eclipsed by the unbelievable complexity of the network and specifically the cells that make up that network.

In each cell is the most complex piece of information we have discovered. It is the DNA molecule on which the human genome is based. The human brain has 10,000 times more storage capacity than the human genome.

Unlike parts of a computer, which are analogs to switches that are either one or off, nerve cells are highly individualized. No two cells are exactly the same, nor do they respond to the same incoming information in the same way. Each neuron is unique in the whole universe. God's creative design comes down to every last neuron in our brain.

In the midst of this complexity, the neurosurgeon comes along with a lifetime of education and training and still he or she stands about a step and a half in front of the witch doctor when treating this fantastic organ. With Hippocratic allegiance, he or she endeavors to "do no harm" first... because they know the design here is far beyond their collective intelligence. The doctors clamp here and add a chemical there but they realize the best they can do is to try to help create a setting for the brain to do what it was created to do, fire and drive all the functions of the body.

We come to agree with the psalmist who said,

> *For You formed my inward parts;*
> *You wove me in my mother's womb.*
> *I will give thanks to You, for I am fearfully and wonderfully made;*
> *Wonderful are Your works, and my soul knows it very well.*
>
> *- Psalm 139:13-14*

So we bring patients like Carol to hospitals like Jefferson, which is ranked #1 in the Nation for Neuroscience, and at the same time we pray to the Creator to superintend her healing. He alone fully understands what has to happen for Carol to get better. He certainly works through doctors, but He also can easily do what they can't.

*(Resource – **More Than Meets the Eye**, Richard Swenson, Navpress, Colorado Springs 2000)*

Day 29 – (Day 22 @ TJUH) Sunday, August 30, 2009

Vision - still improving. Carol read words off a clipboard today.

65

Motor Abilities – She got out of bed today and walked to the doorway and back twice, and sat up in a chair for 3 hours.

Spirits – Carol was really excited about getting out of bed… this is a big step towards getting ready for therapy. Tomorrow the physical therapists will start working with her.

Day 30 – (Day 23 @ TJUH) Monday, August 31, 2009

Vision - still improving. Carol has cuts in her vision which means there are regions she sees very well and other regions where she does not. Her peripheral vision is about 75 degrees from straight ahead on the left and about 40 degrees from straight ahead on the right. She was worked with an occupational therapist today on her depth perception. Her brain is still processing incorrectly up and down on occasion. When she gets tired and has been trying to focus for too long, her eyes start to drift. The doctors say her vision deficits are 100 percent processing issues. The doctors believe as the brain continues to heal that these deficits will shake out in time. No one is guaranteeing anything. We'll keep praying.

Motor Abilities – Carol got out of bed, walked out the doorway and down the hall, came back and sat up in a chair for an hour, with the help of 2 nurses. During meals, I hand Carol a forkful of food and she brings it to her mouth to eat by herself. She wrote her name on a clipboard today.

Spirits – The doctors are talking about transferring Carol to a regular room out of ICU as soon as a bed becomes available. She is ready to get to rehab.

Diagnosis - The diagnosis is still Reversible Cerebral Vasoconstriction Syndrome. Her anti-spasm med, nimodipine, is done. Her vena cava line was removed today, which means she is finished with Neosynepherine. BP is looking good; it is being controlled by an oral medicine. There is an IV port in her arm, but she is not connected to any IV lines! The three things she still has on are a BP cuff that automatically takes her blood pressure every 30 minutes, a heart-rate sensor that tracks the heart waves and a pulse-ox sensor on her finger that measures oxygen level in the blood. Those three things are quickly snapped off when Carol gets ready to walk around.

On Saturday, we looked at the brain, today let's look at the eye. The eye is an organ of unequaled sensitivity, precision, complexity, and beauty. Like everything else God created, the eye is an engineering marvel.

Darwin told a friend, "The eye to this day gives me a cold shudder. To suppose that the eye, with all its inimitable contrivances for adjusting the focus to different distances, for admitting different amounts of light, and for the correction of spherical and chromatic aberration, could have been formed by natural selection, seems, I freely confess, absurd in the highest possible degree." This Darwin said not even realizing the deeper chemical and electrical complexities involved in the eye's operation. This was a rare moment of honesty from the divinity student turned biologist.

Light hits the cornea first, the primary focusing structure... that alone is astounding, the outermost surface of the eye that appears to be just a clear covering carries on the bulk of the focusing job. From there, light passes through the iris, the eye's "shutter," that controls how much light is allowed to enter the eye. The iris is able to contract or dilate depending on the intensity of the incoming light. The iris also gives the eye its blue-green-brown color. The iris has 266 identifiable characteristics and is the most data-rich physical structure in the body, far more unique than a fingerprint which has only 35 measurable characteristics.

One maker of an iris-scanner for computer identification claims the biometric structures are so unique that there is only a 1 in 10^{78} chance that two people's irises will match. Since we only have 6 billion people (or roughly 1×10^{10}) on the earth, the iris scan for identification is virtually dead-on accurate.

Once light passes through the iris/pupil area it enters the lens which additionally focuses light. As light emerges behind the lens it hits the retina, a thin lining in the back of the eye. The retina is composed of photoreceptor cells that are light sensitive, converting the image into electrical signals that can in turn be interpreted by the brain.

A camera takes a picture and develops the image into a form we can look at afterwards. The eye takes pictures continuously and develops and records each image instantaneously – a process we can't stop even if we wanted to. So if we know we have a horrible image in front of us we close our eyes and instinctively cover our faces with our hands so that we don't see and record the image.

On the retina are 120 million rods and 7 million cones. The rods accomplish dim vision, night vision, and peripheral vision. The cones are for color vision and fine detail. Each eye has one million nerve fibers that electrically connect the photoreceptors in the retina to the visual cortex of the brain.

At Jefferson, the neuro-ophthalmologists, after examining Carol, reported that everything from the optic nerve forward was fine – which is to say a lot.

The neural impulses reach the visual cortex of the brain where the image is reconstructed in such a *way that we "see" it. This processing center is where Carol's brain is healing.*

John Stevens writing in the journal <u>Byte</u>, in an article entitled "Reverse Engineering the Brain" wrote,

> *While today's digital hardware is extremely impressive, it is clear that human retina's real-time performance goes unchallenged. Actually, to simulate 10 milliseconds of the complete processing of even a single nerve cell from the retina would require the solution of about 500 simultaneous nonlinear differential equations 100 times and would take at least several minutes of processing time on a Cray supercomputer. Keeping in mind that there are 10 million or more such cells interacting with each other in complex ways, it would take a minimum of 100 years of Cray time to simulate what takes place in your eye many times a second.*

Dr. Swenson writes,

> *"The human eye can distinguish millions of shades of color. On a clear dark night, we can see a small candle flame from 30 miles away. In a lifetime we blink hundreds of millions of times.*

> *Like the brain, there's more about the eye we don't know than we know. Opticians tell us that light can enter the eye and possibly reflect from the eye, but it cannot generate its own light. But if you ever saw the joyful*

*eyes of a small child who just received a
new toy – the physics fails us to explain
what is seen in those eyes at that moment."*

*I have a verse of scripture plastered on a post-it
stuck on my car's dash, the car I drive back and
forth to Jefferson every day that says...*

*The hearing ear and the seeing eye, the
Lord has made both of them (Proverbs
20:12).*

*The Creator who made "the hearing ear" and "the
seeing eye" is uniquely qualified to superintend
their repair. Carol has the best doctors and nurses
in the world – they truly are wonderful gifted people
– down to the very last one, but God's got to touch
her eyes and her brain for her vision to improve.*

*(Resource – **More Than Meets the Eye**, Richard
Swenson, Navpress, Colorado Springs 2000)*

Day 31 – (Day 24 @ TJUH) Tuesday, September 1, 2009

Carol has moved! She is in the same building, the
Gibbon Building, but now in room 9229.

Her room overlooks the beautiful and expansive
atrium that extends from the ground floor to the top
of the building. In fact, if you come up in the atrium
elevators and get off at the 9th floor – you can see
across the atrium and into Carol's room if the
curtains are pulled back. She moved at about 3
p.m. It is a step-down from the Neurological
Intensive Care Unit (NICU).

Motor Abilities – With the aid of a nurse Carol is getting out of bed now and walking around and sitting for longer periods in a chair. She is receiving occupational therapy every day – a great new friend named Nancy is working with her. Maybe she will see the physical therapist tomorrow. During meals, I hand Carol a forkful of food and she brings it to her mouth to eat by herself. Her catheter is coming out tomorrow morning, so she should be able to walk the floor more independently.

Cognitive Abilities – Carol's short-term memory is getting stronger. Her brain function seems to be getting better and better.

Spirits – Every treatment that is eliminated is getting Carol closer to Betty Bacharach Rehabilitation Center. She's excited. Diana Duffy from Betty Bacharach came to see Carol today and said there's a bed at Bacharach and they are just waiting for the doctors to say it's okay to leave Jefferson.

Diagnosis – Her brain function is back to normal. Her BP is being kept slightly higher by an oral medicine.

Thanks for all your prayers and gestures of kindness - please keep approaching the throne of grace.

Morning Thoughts – September 1, 2009

I was reading Mark 2 last night and read again these two verses. Jesus is speaking.

> *And no one sews a patch of unshrunk cloth on an old garment, otherwise the patch pulls away from it, the new from the old, and a worse tear results. And no one puts new wine into old wineskins; otherwise the wine will burst the skins, and the wine is lost, and the skins as well; but one puts new wine into fresh wineskins (Mk.2:21-22).*

The issue Jesus was addressing was how the old conventions tend to burst when God does a new work. The wise among us stay like fresh wineskins, soft and flexible, not rigid and inflexible. The Pharisees always resisted Jesus because they had Israel in a spiritual strait-jacket. They needed grace to stretch and to receive what God had for them.

The same is true today. The God of Creation is always interested in making new creatures out of us and we tend to want to force everyone into a stiff, traditional mode.

An interesting study can be made of comparing what God creates versus what man makes. What God creates is always unique, one of a kind. When man makes something, he tends to mass produce the same thing over and over… like a giant Lego project. This comparison is seen when God demanded His temple be built with stones fit together in which no tool ever touched as opposed to man's building practice of using things like bricks stamped out of a mold. An easy comparison of God's ability versus ours is seen in how we build things. God never makes two things alike… He is the Master Artist.

My friend, Pastor Len Rudderow, and I had many conversations about this passage. Now Len is 85 and he just moved 500 miles to enter an assisted living facility in North Carolina. We agreed that if we want God to pour new wine into us, we must make sure we stay flexible.

During Carol's harrowing August, we have had no choice but to stay flexible. If we clamp down on the idea I just want things to be like they used to be… we will be a lot more like the old wine skin. We will find ourselves bursting at the seams. Life changes! Challenges are brought to us. God wants us to sincerely believe "I can do all things through Christ who strengthens me" (Philippians 4:13).

George

Chapter 6 – Sit, Stay, Heal!

As George and I write this, much of it is news to me. While I have memories of a few events, there is very little frame of reference. Certain "milestones" are etched in my brain. Sitting up for the first time! Standing up for the first time while attached to a multitude of IV's and attempting to walk! And perhaps the most deeply engrained, going to the bathroom! While I was very ill and not aware of much of my surroundings, being catheterized was a major blessing. However, it was made clear to me, I would not be released from Jefferson until I was no longer utilizing a catheter. By this time in my hospitalization, I had not utilized a bathroom in 24 days. Don't let anyone ever tell you, urinating is like riding a bike: once you learn, you never really forget! Not true! So, on the evening prior to my scheduled release to rehabilitation in South Jersey, there I was, unable to utilize the bathroom! Not to be too descriptive of the multitude of methods used in correcting this situation, suffice it to say, think heat lamps, pressure, dipping your hands in warm water, and the all-time favorite, the sound of running water! Coupled with my lack of ability to walk alone, the inability to urinate and the necessity to do so made for a harrowing evening, to say the least. I am not sure for whom it was most harrowing, me the patient, or the poor, yet loving, nursing staff attempting to assist with this endeavor. Success was achieved, not easily however. I do recall the evening ending with me not quite back in the bed and somewhat sunburned but smiling!

Carol

Lucia Brubaker, a good friend for years. Lucy and her husband, Dan, have been missionaries for over 30 years in Mali, a country in western Africa where they have labored for a lifetime to minister to the

Minyankan people and to help them develop a written language, to translate the Bible into their language, to write a dictionary and now to teach this special population how to read their new written language thanks to the Wycliffe Bible Translators. Lucy's note...

This is all wonderful news.

I have the card... a beautiful "hug" card that Carol sent me up on the shelf in front of my desk in the living room. Every day I feel her hug and prayers. Please give her a hug and warm greetings from me, would you?

May the Lord strengthen and bless you, George. Thanks for taking such good care of Carol.

Blessings,
Lucia

Day 32 – (Day 25 @ TJUH) Wednesday, September 2, 2009

Carol has moved again! This time she's moving to Betty Bacharach Rehabilitation Hospital in Galloway Township near Atlanticare Regional Medical Center. We're asking for everyone to hold off on visiting her on the 1st day (Thursday) so Carol isn't inundated. I will pass on the room number tomorrow.

She is being transported this morning via ambulance from Jefferson to Bacharach.

Vision – her vision is still improving. The neurologists Dr. Will Neil and Dr. Jackie Urtecho videotaped Carol's Neurological Exam for a Journal Study on her condition. Again no guarantees, but they seem to indicate that Carol's vision will continue to improve and Dr. Jackie said there is a possibility she may eventually drive again. First things first, Carol's on her way to Bacharach and she will enter an Acute Rehabilitation program. They will be helping her gain better orientation and perception ability and compensations for current deficits. The doctors want to do another videotape in December to document Carol's anticipated improvement. She will have to come back to Jefferson Neuroscience for another angiogram, as an outpatient and receive checkups.

Motor Abilities – Carol was walking the 9th floor yesterday at Jefferson. Her left hand and arm are getting better.

Cognitive Abilities - Her brain function seems to be getting better and better. She is doing better with mental math problems.

Spirits – She is pumped.

Diagnosis – Her brain function is getting back to normal. Her BP is being kept slightly higher by an oral medicine.

Keep praying.

Morning Thoughts – September 2, 2009

Remember the verse I shared yesterday?

> *And no one sews a patch of unshrunk cloth on an old garment, otherwise the patch pulls away from it, the new from the old, and a worse tear results. And no one puts new wine into old wineskins; otherwise the wine will burst the skins, and the wine is lost, and the skins as well; but one puts new wine into fresh wineskins. (Mark 2:21-22)*

The Lord shares here to be prepared for changes that God brings we must stay flexible and not rigid. To be sure, there was no one who was more of a stickler about the truth than Jesus Christ. He often pointed out, that men make their mistakes because they do not understand the Scriptures. (Matthew 22:29) So when we seek to be flexible, the Lord is not talking about being soft and flexible on the truth. He was referring to the idea of holding the truth on one hand but being flexible in understanding that God works in many ways, often very unpredictable ways on the other. After all we are dealing with a God of infinite intelligence. Are His ways going to transcend our thinking? Undoubtedly!

Listen to way the prophet Isaiah puts it, he says thus says the Lord…

> *For as the heavens are higher than the earth, so are my ways higher than your ways, and my thoughts than your thoughts. (Isaiah 55:9)*

78

So, the truth is God loves us and deserves our love back. We reflect His love by loving others. He will never leave us nor forsake us. And He is working out every circumstance that comes into our lives for a good purpose (Romans 8:28). He desires for us to remember that, so we would be blessed and He would be glorified. That's the truth. How God does that... is His job.

So, in our lives, when we have more twists and turns than a bobsled run, we can stand by faith on His Word... and we can flex. God's love is what gives us the power to stand strong in the midst of adversity. He is still sitting on the throne. There hasn't been a palace coup in heaven that has led to Carol's condition, so we all must stay strong and flex with every turn. We have no choice and more specifically, I have no other choice. I have to handle what is coming up next, by His grace, for the woman I love.

George

Once again, I must admit I have little or no recollection of my ambulance ride to Bacharach. I am convinced the Lord spared me from remembering my series of transports. If you know me well, you are aware of the fact I am high maintenance! Preparing for ANYTHING that involves me going somewhere always involved make-up, a lot of make-up, electric curlers (yes, they still make them), and a large purse full of other essentials! None of which I had for any of my moves! This trip was me in a hospital gown, wrapped in blankets, and fairly in "La-La Land." Upon arrival, I was placed in a hallway to await an available room. Lying there watching people pass, upside down, I was searching each face for George's.

Suddenly, a woman passed, slowed, turned around and grabbed my arm. It was Terry Esposito, our Wells Fargo financial advisor. She grabbed my arm and smiled and said she would be praying for me. Once again, I ask, what are the chances! Not chance, an all-knowing God preparing my way! Shortly after my encounter with Terry, another familiar face appeared!

Now readers, if you recall the nurse, Kelly, who comforted me prior to my aborted helicopter ride, you should thank the Lord for your memory! (And know that I am confessing jealously at this moment!) If you don't remember, join the club and let me assist you. Kelly is a friend, a nurse, who comforted and encouraged me on the night I was admitted to the hospital, 31 days prior! Now, not in the middle of the night, not in the Emergency Room, here she was again! She stopped, grabbed my arm and told me she would be around to check on me once I was settled in. New hospital, new surroundings, same, unchanging, solid Rock! I breathed a sigh of relief and continued my search for George, my other source of refuge and love.

Carol

Day 33 – (Day 1 @ BBRH) Thursday, September 3, 2009

Carol is at Bacharach! She is in Room 19B in the A-wing.

Vision - Carol will have to come back to Jefferson Neuroscience for another angiogram as an outpatient and will have vision checkups at Bacharach.

Motor Abilities – Carol's physical therapy and occupational therapy, and acute therapy at Bacharach start tomorrow. Her left hand and arm are getting better.

Spirits – She still is pumped.

Keep praying.

Morning Thoughts – September 3, 2009

As Carol leaves Jefferson this morning to go the Betty Bacharach Rehabilitation Hospital, I'm thinking about all the doctors and staff at Jefferson Neuroscience and Jefferson Hospital who helped Carol so much. I'm thanking God for each one and asking His best for them.

These are the ones I remember and I know I forgot a few.

Neuro Doctors *- Dr. Pascal Jabbour, Dr. Will Neil, Dr. Ciro Randazzo, Dr. Rohan Chitale, Dr. Valerie DeChant, Dr. Michael Moussouttas, Dr. Jackie Urtecho and Dr. Rodney Bell*

Nurses *– Nick, Pat, Sonja, Jenny, Jenna, Tamika, Judy, Lori, Bridget, Alison, Tony, Cheryl, Ching, Karen, Melissa and Amy*

Technician *– Joe, Gretchen*

Doppler Technicians *– Terri, Karen*

Occupational Therapist *- Nancy*

25 days of getting Carol better – each one of these professionals will be held close in our hearts.

George

Chapter 7 - Allen & Wendy

Even on this evening, October 26, 2017, as I begin to write about my experience with the team of therapists at Bacharach, I am deeply moved and eternally thankful for each and every one of them. While I mention Allen and Wendy by name and am especially grateful to them for their contribution to my recovery, every person with whom I came in contact at this remarkable facility has a special place in my heart. As you read this story, please know that the work of rehabilitation is a lifesaving work and those who take part in it are truly in the business of restoring lives. From the administrators who work diligently to admit patients to the kind souls who clean the rooms at night, they are all helping an interrupted life slowly be put back together. When I was fully, (well as fully as I was going to get!) recovered, I strongly contemplated returning to school and studying physical and or occupational therapy. It truly meant that much to me. If you are a therapist or are contemplating becoming one, please know you do have the capacity and ability to remarkably alter lives! Thank you, one and all!

Carol

Day 34 – (Day 2 @ BBRH) Friday, September 4, 2009

Vision - There are still some parts of her field of vision where she doesn't see as well. Her ability to orient to her surroundings is getting better even in a brand-new setting. She is going to meet with a neuro-ophthalmologist on September 15 who will make his recommendations for therapy.

Occupational Therapy – Carol's occupational therapist is Allen. He helped her to dress herself in street clothes in the morning. Allen told Carol that therapy will take some time. He said the typical formula is for every day a patient is lying in a hospital bed and not able to get up translates into five days of therapy. Carol was in a Jefferson bed for 23 consecutive days before she started to get up – that means a realistic recovery therapy time will be 115 days – about 4 months.

Allen spent most of his OT time with having Carol stand up from chairs and bed-like surfaces and negotiating getting in and out of different places. He had her get into and out of an automobile driver's seat. He helped her into and out of a bathtub and a walk-in shower. He worked on her left thumb and hand – stretching the fingers and the hand. He helped her to better point with her index finger and to start to raise her left thumb.

Physical Therapy – Carol's main physical therapist is Wendy. Wendy is ably assisted by an intern named Anthony. They assessed Carol's ability to stand, roll over in a bed, walk with a walker and measured the range of motion for all her moving joints. They got Carol up and had her walk. Her leg muscles are weak from lying in bed… so it is difficult for her to stand – she must really push with her legs. Once she is standing – her balance is good, and she can walk well.

Speech/Cognitive Therapy – The speech therapist saw Carol and said that obviously there are no speech deficits, so she took her hour to assess cognitive and memory deficits. There are still areas of minor confusion, but her memory is already better than mine. Occasionally, she misses a fact she should have remembered – but it is amazing how much better her thinking is.

Walking Tour with Wendy - In the afternoon Carol had to do laps in the gym at Bacharach. Wendy helped Carol in getting up and down and walking the course with her. Her gait was a little narrow, like she was walking a tight rope, so Wendy talked to her about widening her gait. Carol did that and her walking began to look better.

Carol was told that she could see pets – but they must be kept outside because the Bacharach staff had to deal recently with a dog bite of a patient. Of course, Ashley, our golden retriever, has absolutely no idea how that would be done. Carol and Ashley will have some time together on Saturday.

Keep praying.

At Bacharach, many of my fellow patients were recovering from hip and knee replacements. In light of this fact, I was one of the youngest patients on the wing. We would be awakened at six in the morning in order for the nurses and aides to have us up and ready for breakfast and therapy. Those of us who could walk with assistance, me included, were usually attended to after those patients who needed more intensive care. Consequently, I would be one of the last to be assisted into the bathroom. My aide and I would walk with the walker into the bathroom and I would be seated on the raised toilet. Bearing in mind I could not leave the bed without assistance, I did not want to bother anyone during the night to help me to the bathroom, and we were in bed by nine, I was more than ready to use the facilities by the time it was my turn! One morning while I was relieving myself, my aide said to me in a matter-of-fact manner, "You pee like a race horse!" I chose to take it as a compliment!!

Carol

A custom George started in the evenings after dinner at Bacharach was to take me for a spin in the wheelchair around the facilities. Later, as I improved, we would walk the halls before he left. One evening early in my stay, George was pushing me around. He stopped at a corner and asked me which way he should turn to return to my room. I looked at the arrows on the wall and told him which way. We repeated this for a few other corners. After returning to my room, George informed me I had been in error with all of the directions! This was the beginning of how we would discover some of the long lasting, if not permanent, effects of the brain injury. I, of course, was discouraged, but not too upset, assuming by the time I left Bacharach, I would be fine. George, however, did not share that opinion, but thankfully kept it to himself.

Carol

As Carol described this revelation, I would add we would come to an intersection in the hall where we could only go forward or left, and I asked Carol, "Look at the arrow (which was pointing left) and tell me which way should we turn to go back to the room." She pointed to the right which was an exterior wall. My silent reaction was "Oh boy!" That was the first hint that directions, left and right, were going to be a challenge.

Morning Thoughts – September 4, 2009

There's an old quote that "laughter is the best medicine." How old? Well… at least 3000 years. The proverb written by Solomon, King David's son is about 3000 years old. It is translated in our English Bible,

> *"A merry heart does good like a medicine." (Proverbs 17:22)*

There are three verses in the book of "Proverbs" that deal with a happy, joyful heart. Our verse above and two others – "A merry heart makes a cheerful face." (Proverbs 15:13) and "He that has a merry heart has a continual feast." (Proverbs 15:15)

The Bible teaches how one comes to acquire a merry heart. Salvation brings joy.

> *"I will joy in the God of my salvation." (Habakkuk 3:18)*

There is joy in us when God's Word lives there. Jesus said…

"These things I have spoken to you, that My joy may be in you, and that your joy may be full." There is joy in answered prayer. (Can I hear an amen from those who have been praying for Carol?) Jesus said, "Until now you have asked for nothing in My name; ask and you will receive, that your joy may be full." (John 16:24) There is joy in active faith. Paul writes, "The God of hope fill you with all joy and peace in believing." (Romans 15:13) There is the joy that is part of the fruit of the

Spirit. The fruit (the outworking of the Spirit's presence) is

> *"Love, JOY, peace, patience, kindness, goodness, faithfulness, gentleness, self-control..." (Galatians 5:22-23).*

There is the joy of leading someone to Christ, as Paul spoke of when he referred to the believers at Philippi as "my joy and my crown". (Phil.4:1) There is the joy of being tested and enduring it with God's help –

> *"Count it all joy when you encounter various trials knowing that the testing of your faith produces endurance." (James 1:2-3)*

And there's the supreme joy of knowing and loving the Lord Jesus Christ.

> *"Whom having not seen, you love; in whom, though now you do not see Him, yet believing, you rejoice with joy unspeakable and full of glory." (I Peter 1:8)*

With this God-given joy in our hearts, there is no wonder that there are visible results in our lives. A happy look, a satisfied heart and a positive influence on others all flow from God's joy within.

George

Chapter 8 - Ashley Comes for a Visit!

For anyone who is a pet owner, you know the joy of unconditional love! The day Ashley came to see me in Bacharach, she had no knowledge of the fact I couldn't walk, dress, bathe, eat, read or write without assistance; nor did she care! I was in her presence and I was me, and that was all she cared about. I was thrilled to see and smell her! She brought me joy and comfort.

Unconditional love is an amazing thing, isn't it? While we recognize it in our pets, and to a degree, in our parents, it is even more remarkable to recognize it as THE point of contact with the creator of our universe! If you have experienced the unconditional love of a pet, I implore you to seek out and experience the unconditional love of Jesus Christ. His love and His salvation are available for you and to you just because you are you! His beloved Son gave His life in order for you to spend eternity in heaven with His Father. Accept Jesus as your Savior today and know an unconditional love that will put even my dear, dear Ashley's to shame!

Carol

In preparation for Ashley's trip to see Carol, I took our furry friend to our dog groomer, Beth Simon at the Pet Salon. They are the best and for this grooming there would be absolutely no charge!

George

Here is Beth's contribution – our good friend and dog groomer for decades at the Pet Salon with her husband, Chuck, in Margate, New Jersey

Hi Guys... I miss you tooooooo much!!!!!! I spoke with Deana (one of Beth's grooming techs) about your request (that is for her recollections) and we are not sure what you're looking for. Our memory... is visiting at rehab (at Bacharach Rehabilitation) and at that point you were on the mend and seeing you with Ashley... of course there was fear, concern, but mostly hope for recovery.

Love, Beth Simon

Day 35 – (Day 3 @ BBRH) Saturday, September 5, 2009

Carol's best visit – I don't want to offend any of our human visitors but I'm gonna have to. Carol had her best visit of all those who have come to see her. Her caller was furry and energetic and slobbered a lot... ASHLEY – Carol's Golden Retriever. Beth Simons at the Pet Salon gave her a full grooming, so Ashley never looked or smelled better – and Beth wouldn't take a nickel. I don't know who was more excited Carol or Ashley. They had a good 20 minutes of loving on each other at a picnic area outside Carol's building. That made Carol's day, week and month!

Vision - Carol is reading words from a marker board and starting to write. She must try to track moving objects better. She tends to lose the object she's trying to track visually and focus on other things in the background. We are working on that. She is going to meet with an neuro-ophthalmologist on September 15 who will make his recommendations for therapy.

Walking Tour – 10:30 Carol did laps in the gym at Bacharach. Her walking is getting better each day. She is standing more easily too.

Motor Skills – Carol's pointing better with her left index finger and she's starting to raise that left thumb on her own.

Keep praying!

Morning Thoughts – September 5, 2009

One of Carol's favorite songs is "Let the Lower Lights Be Burning". Carol's family is loaded with sailors. Her dad signed up for the U.S. Navy at the outset of World War II and sailed and fought for our country throughout the Pacific. He loved fishing and taking boats out into the ocean and bays near Atlantic City.

Carol's brother, Ronnie, was a commercial fisherman from his teenage years – became a yacht captain and now builds the best ocean fishing yachts in the world for Sea Force 9 – a company he runs in Southwest Florida. Carol's nephew, Ron, Jr. is a boat captain who ran the Laura Marie fishing boats for years out of New Jersey locales like Ocean City, Somers Point, and Cape May – he and his brother Jeff are now in Florida helping dad at Sea Force 9.

Carol and her sister Evie love taking boat rides and walking/shelling the beaches of Florida and New Jersey. The Rookstools are of Dutch and German extraction so I'm sure there are plenty of salty dogs in their distant past. My dad was a sailor too – he was in the merchant marines in World War II.

The song "Let the Lower Lights Be Burning" is a gospel song about how God saves lost souls like he saves lost boatmen. He uses lighthouses and the men who keep the lamps burning to guide "the poor, fainting, struggling seaman" to harbor and God uses Christians to be His lighthouses to guide struggling sinners to heaven. The verses go as follows:

92

Brightly beams our Father's mercy from His lighthouse evermore,
But to us He gives the keeping of the lights along the shore.

Dark the night of sin has settled, loud the angry billows roar;
Eager eyes are watching, longing, for the lights along the shore.

Trim your feeble lamp, my brother! Some poor sailor tempest-tossed
Trying now to make the harbor, in the darkness may be lost

CHORUS
Let the lower lights be burning! Send a gleam across the wave!
Some poor fainting, struggling seaman you may rescue, you may save.

Today we have GPSes and guided, computer-generated courses. But in the old days, a sailor knew his way from the "lower lights". The upper lights, of course, were the stars and moon above, but the lower lights were on the shore generally, but more specifically the lighthouses where the watchmen would keep the lamps trimmed and burning. Without the faithfulness of those manning the lighthouses, the sailors on a stormy night had no hope of making shore. It's the light that saved the sailor. For those who know Jesus, we have the same responsibility to keep our lamps trimmed and burning – our witness of how God saves people who place their faith in Christ.

"For God so loves the world that He gave His only uniquely-born Son that whosoever believes in Him shall not perish but have eternal life." (John 3:16)

Jesus said,

"I am the Light of the world; he who follows Me shall not walk in darkness but shall have the light of life." (John 8:12)

Someday you'll have to hear Carol sing the song!

George

Day 36 – (Day 4 @ BBRH) Sunday, September 6, 2009

Carol had another visit from Ashley.

Walking Tour – No therapy today – weekend crew – Carol and I went out and walked on a patio near the Cafeteria at meal times.

Motor Skills – Carol's pointing better with her left index finger and she's starting to raise that left thumb on her own.

Keep praying!

Day 37 – (Day 5 @ BIR – Bacharach Institute for Rehab.) Monday – Labor Day, September 7, 2009

Vision - still improving. Carol had an eye-exam today – the doctor was surprised at how many things Carol could see clearly. Depth perception and field cuts are still the major deficits. We want to thank God for the progress so far. She is going

94

to meet with a neuro-ophthalmologist on September 15th who will make his recommendations for therapy.

Physical Therapy – She worked with a therapist by the name of Apollo. His family is from the Philippines. She climbed stairs today and did toe-raisers from a standing position. Of course, she did laps.

Motor Skills – Carol's pointing better with her left index finger and she's starting to raise that left thumb on her own. Carol's walking more and spending less time in the wheelchair.

The full team of therapists will be in tomorrow, so Carol will be back to her 4 hours of therapy.

The full rehab team normally meets on Tuesdays, but because of the holiday this week, it will be Wednesday. At that time the doctors, nurses, therapists and case workers sit down and evaluate each patient to determine his or her progress and decide which ones will be going home this week and who will need another week.

Dr. Alfaro, Carol's doctor, has hinted at maybe recommending Carol be sent home and finishing her rehab as an out-patient.

We will pray!

George

On the morning of my sixth full day at Bacharach, Allen, my Occupational Therapist, came into the room bright and early and casually asked me to get myself dressed! Prior to my brain injury, this would have been a slight challenge. I have always laid my clothes out the night before work to make sure they matched, and were ironed At this juncture; this was a monumental, if not near impossible request. George had picked and packed all the clothes I had at Bacharach. I was fairly certain the clothes were not ironed and definitely certain they did not match! It was at this point, I experienced a startling and clarifying moment. My life, as I knew it, would never be the same!

The simple task of getting dressed on my own would take effort - real effort. And so would everything else I had done without thought for the past 50 years! This became reality when I attempted to put on my bra! Without going into gruesome detail, suffice it to say, picture Houdini escaping from the straight jacket without the underwater tank. Allen, to his credit, remained calm and straight faced throughout the ordeal. That night George was tasked with finding a bra that did not have adjustable straps or hook and eye closures. Our dear friend Joelle was instrumental in making it possible for him to do so.

Carol

Day 38 – (Day 6 @ BIR – Bacharach Institute for Rehab.) Tuesday, September 8, 2009

> Vision - still improving. Carol is seeing smaller print. It's amazing. She still has significant depth-perception issues. She said that she was mentally thinking about how to write numbers today, which is s good step cognitively. The doctors took her BP in bed, sitting up and standing to see if she was ready to be backed off the med that kept her pressure up slightly. She passed the test, so she will be coming off that med. They have stopped

her Cipro. Every med she comes off means she is that much closer to coming home.

The full team of therapists was in today and Carol was back to her 4 hours of work.

Physical Therapy – Carol had a good session with the physical therapists. She's climbing stairs, doing laps – walking much better with almost no assistance and her orientation in the movements is getting much better. Carol really loves Wendy, her therapist.

Occupational Therapy – The OT worked on Carol getting in and out of the mock car, in and out of a shower stall and stretching exercises for the left hand and arm. Carol had to button and fold shirts.

Allen put a stack of Carol's clothes on her tray table and said, "Today, you are going to dress yourself!" Carol was panicked but did it! Prior to this day, someone had to help her get dressed each day.

The full rehab team meets tomorrow to discuss each patient's status and whether Carol can go home.

God has been good; let's keep coming to Him.

Morning Thoughts – September 8, 2009

This morning I'm thinking about the thoughtfulness of so many who have helped us during this difficult time. The cards, gifts, balloons, baked goods and flowers number into the hundreds – not to mention the stream of visitors, phone calls and thoughtful e-mails. Carol and I have felt throughout the weeks that we have never been alone. Of course, Doctor Jesus never left her bedside, but the mortals here on earth have been well-represented, also. It has been interesting to see how many doctors and nurses and hospital staff members have poked their heads in on their off-hours to see how Carol was doing.

Everyone has offered any assistance needed. I have no idea how many people have come over to the house to walk Ashley, our golden retriever – It's been a lot. There are very few nights that there isn't a meal waiting for me when I get home. And my lawn and yard have never looked better. It looks like a golf course. I understand there are guys showing up at the same time to cut the grass, so one mows the grass while the other one trims and edges.

We have people contacting us from across the country and around the world who are praying for Carol. People we met in Colorado at Wind River Ranch are praying for Carol every day. God has been so good.

Our employers have been great too.

Carol's supervisor at Stockton University, Fran Bottone, has said, of course Carol has a ton of sick time – because she never took any sick days. And she said when that runs out; the people at Stockton are lining up to donate their sick time for Carol. She said they have the semester covered and we'll see what happens then. A Vice President of the College, Thomasa Gonzalez, (an old-time friend of Carol's) came today and said not to worry about anything but getting better and that her friends at Stockton are all praying for her.

My supervisor at Atlantic City High School, Sherry Yahn, has set up a substitute to cover the whole month of September. Whatever days I can make it in will save some of my leave time. The substitute teacher she got me is a retired physics professor – he has a Ph.D in physics from the University of Maryland. He taught physics for 45 years at Rutgers University, Camden. He told me he taught the course I teach 43 times. Do you know what a small number of people are qualified to teach AP Physics? And then out of that number, how many are available to take over a class on short notice? That alone is a miracle. Today is the first day of class so I'm going in to meet my students and tell them how things will go until Carol is home and stable.

Our church family has been outstanding too – a hundred kind acts and gestures of love. E-prayers and updates are constantly going out on the Internet.

There has been so much giving in the time of our need, it's hard to say thank you to so many. I hope everyone realizes how much we appreciate all that has been done.

George

Day 39 – (Day 7 @ BIR – Bacharach Institute for Rehabilitation) Wednesday, September 9, 2009

The full rehab team met today. They decided to keep Carol for another week. They said I could take her home if I wanted, but their recommendation was that she stay for another week. Their rationale was that even though medically she could start an outpatient regimen, they felt with her continuing visual problems and her general difficulty with orientation that maybe in the home environment she might find it too difficult and start declining. Carol was disappointed, but after she blew off some steam, she came around to believing that maybe it's for the best. Her vision and orientation are getting better every day. Perhaps next week would be a better time – she will be a week stronger, her vision will be a week better and her ability to orient to being home will also be a week better.

George

Devastated. . . that is the word that best described how I felt when Allen told me I would not be going home. . . devastated. I cried, right in front of him. I tried to hold back the tears, but they came flowing out with each word I tried to say. For those of you who know me, you know I am not a public crier. And to cry in front of Allen, one of my heroes was unthinkable. He was wonderful. He spoke quietly and gently and consoled me. What made it worse was I knew what he was saying was true. I was probably not ready to go home. The thought of another week away from George and undergoing more therapy was disheartening to say the least. When George came that night, I cried even more!

Carol

Vision - still improving. Evie, Carol's sister, spoke with the vision expert at her school and she recommended trying some strategies for reading. One is to cover up the lines above and below where Carol's trying to read so she can focus on one line at a time. Another suggested strategy is when Carol gets to a place where she can't see the rest of a line, she is to turn her head slightly in that direction to view the part she is having difficulty seeing. My sister-in-law, Carol, had printed out scripture verses in 70-point fonts to use when Carol was ready to try reading. Up to this point Carol has said, "I can't really see that." She could pick up a word here or there. Tonight, Evie helped her read out loud "O give thanks for He is good: for His mercy endureth forever." (Psalm 107:1) She also read Psalm 26:3 and Psalm 46:1. She is officially starting to read!

The full team of therapists was in today for her 4 hours of work.

Physical Therapy – Carol had a good session with the physical therapists. She is climbing stairs, doing laps – walking much better with almost no assistance and her orientation in the movements is getting much better.

Occupational Therapy – The occupational therapist worked with having Carol lie down on the floor and having her practice getting herself to standing up. It was difficult, but she was able to do it. He had

101

her bend her knees and then push up on her toes several times in a row and then he said "jump" and after a few tries, she jumped – her vertical was as bad as mine, but she did jump several times.

The Walking Tour – Carol and I walked together for about a half an hour. She also walked on a treadmill for 15 minutes. Carol is considered now fully ambulatory. She can walk with me through the halls of the hospital. We took advantage of that last night… a long walk… it was good.

Her diagnosis was Reversible Cerebral Vasoconstriction Syndrome. The most beautiful word in that fifty cent term is "Reversible"! We see it every day. Carol is getting better and recovery abilities that have been closed off to her for the last month.

Keep praying!

Morning Thoughts – September 9, 2009

Psalm 23 has been a favorite of God's people for 30 centuries.

> The Lord is my shepherd; I shall not want. He makes me to lie down in green pastures; he leads me beside still waters. He restores my soul; he leads me in the paths of righteousness for his name's sake. Yea, though I walk through the valley of the shadow of death, I will fear no evil; for Thou art with me; thy rod and thy staff they comfort me. Thou preparest a table before me in the presence of mine enemies; thou anointest my head with oil; my cup runneth over. Surely goodness and mercy shall follow me all the days of my life; and I will dwell in the house of the Lord forever.

The key to understanding the Shepherd's Psalm is found in the fourth word... The Lord is MY shepherd.

The world is full of people who are comfortable with generalized, indefinite references to God. We are never really ready to speak intelligently about the Lord until we can say, "The Lord is MY Shepherd". When we own Him as our Shepherd, we also commit ourselves to the wonderful things He does for His sheep. The green pastures and the still waters (His nourishing Word), the restored soul (His indwelling Spirit), the paths of righteousness (His gentle, precious guidance) – all are ours when we come to say and mean "MY Shepherd".

Even at that, our relationship with God can still be somewhat theoretical and academic. It is only when we sense the presence of our dear Shepherd in the valley of the shadow of death that we can cling to the thought "Thou art with me."

Even when there are no still waters, no refreshment and seemingly no shining pathway of guidance – only gloom, threats, and dire predictions – our trusting heart can rest at the darkest hour in His promise "Thou art with me." As a result, faith bumps fear and we discover the truth that we can honestly say "I will fear no evil!" God's rod and staff comfort us because we know Who watches and cares for us in the deepest ravine.

We need to make the transition from an indefinite, impersonal relationship with God to that of a committed love to the One who is worthy of all our trust.

George

Day 40 – (Day 8 @ BIR – Bacharach Institute for Rehabilitation) Thursday, September 10, 2009

The full team of therapists was in today for Carol's 4 hours of work.

Physical Therapy – Carol had a good session with the physical therapists. She's climbing stairs, doing laps – walking much better with almost no assistance and her orientation in the movements is getting much better.

Occupational Therapy – They had me do the stairs, ramp, street curbs and mock car with Carol so when she leaves I'll be able to help her to navigate those places. Today Carol was working on independence around the house in the kitchen and other house settings. Allen took Carol outside and had her walk on different and uneven surfaces and she did fine.

The Walking Tour – We walked with no physical contact. She is doing most of her normal tasks independently.

Keep praying!

Day 41 – (Day 9 @ BIR – Bacharach Institute for Rehab.)
Friday, September 11, 2009

Cognitive Therapy – Susan worked with Carol on memory and general awareness of surroundings. She is doing well in both areas.

Physical Therapy – Carol climbed 15 stairs with Anthony. She is walking without being led. Her gait is almost back to normal.

Occupational Therapy – Bacharach has a mock kitchen, bathroom, living room and laundry room. Carol is working on walking independently in those rooms and completing assignments that her therapist assigns her to do.

The Walking Tour – A ton of walking. I took Carol out to parking lot – she spotted my car from 30 feet away. (That was our chance to make a run for it!)

Vision – There are so many things Carol can see very well. However she still has a problem with how the different images she sees go together and there are blind spots in which she still is not seeing well – down and to the right is one of them.

She has come so far. We will continue to do what we can and trust God for what we cannot!

Chapter 9 - Field Trip... "Don't Tell Them I Fell!"

Day 42 – (Day 10 @ BIR – Bacharach Institute for Rehab.) Saturday, September 12, 2009

FIELD TRIP – We got the OK to take Carol on Field Trip tomorrow. They call it a Therapeutic Home Visit (THV). I will eat breakfast with Carol at Bacharach and then take her home for the day. We have to be back for dinner at 5:00 PM. It should be a lot of fun!

Physical Therapy – Carol walked a lot.

Occupational Therapy – Carol worked on seeing things and picking them up. Claire spread out a series of playing cards on a table and had Carol pick up the cards for which she asked. She had to put a series of cards in the same suits that were spread on a table in order from lowest to highest. She is going to be ready to play solitaire soon.

Vision – Carol has an appointment with the neuro-ophthalmologist Tuesday.

CT Scan at Jefferson Neuroscience Hospital on Thursday, September 24th at 11:00 AM. This will be Carol's first trip back to Jefferson since being discharged on September 3rd. We have a follow up visit with Dr. Bell scheduled for November 11 – that's the earliest appointment – we are trying to move it up.

She has come so far.

One of the points of wisdom God brings us slowly to understand is that He has an unbelievable way of turning cursing into blessing. We look at a circumstance and when we add it up, we think in our finite minds what God has allowed can never bring blessing and yet in time we see His hand. We realize His wisdom is always greater than ours.

I'm thinking about King David this morning. When David asked his cabinet to start a census to count the people – David's motive was impure. Now a census in and of itself is not wrong. In fact, God commanded Moses to conduct a census in his day. What was wrong was David's motive? The Shepherd King was making a statement about how many fighting men he had as king in Israel and Judah. The numbers turned out to be 800,000 in Israel (the northern tribes) and 500,000 in Judah (the southern tribes). And David clearly implied and believed through this census that these numbers were where his comfort and confidence resided. From a human perspective, an army of 1.3 million is very impressive. From God's perspective, David was saying that now his strength was in his army. God made David king of Israel – David didn't. God blessed David's battles with all the Goliaths he faced in his life. And now, David could try to forget God and claim his strength was in numbers. How foolish! The only thing that is sadder is how we who have David's bad example are so like David in our failures.

When David commanded Joab to take this census, Joab responded:

"Now may the Lord your God add to the people a hundred times as many as they are, while the eyes of my lord the king still see; but why does my lord the king delight in this thing?" (2 Samuel 24:3)

David was determined.

"Nevertheless, the king's word prevailed against Joab and against the commanders of the army. So Joab and the commanders of the army went out from the presence of the king to register the people of Israel" (2 Samuel 24:4).

David's decision reveals two things about his personal life at this time. First, he was out of touch with the Lord. We don't read anywhere here of David praying, seeking God's counsel or talking to the prophets that God had provided to help him in his decision-making. He simply decided to do it. Second, he was unaccountable to anyone around him. By dismissing Joab, apparently not even answering his question, the "mighty" king of Israel showed him who was boss. The big problem with that was Joab was right and David was wrong! My brother-in-law, Carol's brother Ronnie, has a saying that hangs in his plant, "It's not who's right, it's what's right!"

David's on the edge of making a huge mistake that will bring dire consequences to the country he loves. But as I suggested in the first paragraph, God has a way of, by His grace, turning even our defeats into something He can bless… even if it's just a bad example to be avoided.

Day 43 – (Day 11 @ BIR – Bacharach Institute for Rehab.) Sunday, September 13, 2009

FIELD TRIP – Carol came home for a Field Trip today. We ate breakfast at Bacharach and then I brought her home for the day. We were back for dinner at 5:00 PM. It was a lot of fun!

We arrived home at 9:30 AM. Carol loved walking into the house. Ashley was the greeting committee! We sat and relaxed. Carol loves the TV series Monk – so we watched an episode on our big screen. She enjoyed that.

We went to lunch around 11:00. We wanted to go to Town & Country, a local restaurant in our Egg Harbor Township. We got there and we saw a waiting line – so we went to Applebee's in Somers Point. They just opened so we got a table right away. Carol ordered Chicken Tenders with French Fries and I got a hamburger. It was great to eat out with her.

We came home. We relaxed in the living room. A few people came over to say hi – my brother John and his wife Carol and their children – our friends Bob and Lily Haws and their daughter Catherine, who had come from Ohio for a wedding stopped by– Roseann, Carol's good friend from work and her daughter, Kaitlyn and our good friend, DJ.

Before we had to go back to Bacharach, Carol, DJ and I watched an episode of another show Carol likes, *Psych*. It was funny and we laughed a lot. We got back to Bacharach at 5 p.m. for dinner. We talked about a few things I could install before she comes home for good. I stayed until they kicked me out at the end of visiting hours. We had a wonderful day! Thank you, Lord!

George

I wish I had written down everything that we did on that day trip! I wish I could have written at that point! Being at home with George and Ashley was so wonderful and so comforting. Seeing our dear friends and family in our home was like a dream. It was something I had taken for granted for so many years, but now it is a new reality for me. It is at times like these, people, me included, say they will never take routine things for granted again. However, time moves on, life moves on, and we do as well. Perhaps one of the reasons the Lord allows incalculable interruptions to enter our lives is to have us stop just long enough to focus on Him and the multitude of blessings of which we partake daily. I encourage you to stop right now and count your many blessings.

I so loved the trip home! However, it made contemplating the return to therapy even more daunting. I was determined to keep all the rules so as not to in any way endanger my chances of being released permanently. If you know me, I never met a rule I didn't like! We were careful to not over-do it. We were careful in the car and around the house. We held hands while walking, especially outside. We were preparing to come back into the house from our last stroll before returning to Bacharach when the unthinkable happened. I attempted to walk up the two stone steps in the front of the house when I lost my balance and… sat down hard! George hurriedly helped me up. We looked at each other and said simultaneously, "Don't tell them I fell down!" And up to the reading of this sentence, it has been our secret!

Vision – Carol has an appointment with the Neuro-Ophthalmologist Tuesday.

CT Scan at Jefferson Neuroscience Hospital on Thursday, September 24 at 11:00 a.m. This will be Carol's first trip back to Jefferson since being discharged on September 3. We have a follow up visit with Dr. Bell scheduled for November 11. This is the earliest appointment – we are trying to move it up.

Pray for God to do what we can't do – heal Carol.

Day 44 – (Day 12 @ BIR – Bacharach Institute for Rehab.) Monday, September 14, 2009

The rehab staff told Carol today that she will soon be leaving Bacharach – it's just a matter of which day. The team meets tomorrow to decide when she will go home. The only thing is that there is a different set of therapists who do outpatient therapy – so Carol will be working with new people when she comes home. She seems to be okay with that even though she has gotten very close to her current therapists.

Physical Therapy – Carol's getting In and out of the mock car went smoothly. She is walking better and better. Today they had her run in the halls. She also tried running up the steps. After 12 days of therapy she is running in the halls – not bad.

Occupational Therapy – Her eye-hand coordination is getting better. She is performing more of the day-to day things she will have to do when she gets home.

Vision – Carol has an appointment with the neuro-ophthalmologist tomorrow. She seems to be seeing a lot more things. She still has trouble with seeing the field down and to her right.

Walking Tour – Today Carol did a half hour on the treadmill. She also rode a stationary bike for 10 minutes.

We thank God for the progress and are asking God to continue what He does – heal.

Morning Thoughts – September 14, 2009

It's 5 a.m. – I just finished Carol's update and I'm getting ready to go to work. I want to continue the thoughts I started Saturday.

God loves turning cursing into blessing. David, driven by selfish pride, orders his commanders to number the people. His top advisor, Joab, essentially asks the question, "Why would you want to do that?" His point was God continues to bless Israel – numbering the people would only be David's way of saying how great David was. The tally was 1.3 million fighting men in Israel and Judah. David liked that number. David's arrogance showed that he was out of touch with God and felt he was unaccountable to anybody.

God allowed David to number the people and then He judged the nation for their king's action. God always holds His own to a higher standard. 70,000 of David's men were taken in a pestilence. David wanted to work with numbers – this turned out to be painful arithmetic. God was sending an angel to destroy Jerusalem when it says in God's Word,

> *"David's heart troubled him after he had numbered the people. So David said to the Lord, 'I have sinned greatly in what I have done. But now, O Lord, please take away the iniquity of Thy servant, for I have acted foolishly.'" (2 Samuel 24:10)*

David was a great king in Israel not because he was always right, because he clearly wasn't, but because he was willing to admit when he was wrong and to seek God's forgiveness.

114

At that moment, God could have taken David's life and all his countrymen, but he gave him a message instead. He said:

> "Go up and build an altar to the Lord on the threshing floor of Ornan the Jebusite." (I Chronicles 21:18)

Ornan was not a Jew but he owned a piece of property that would become extremely important to God's people.

This was the site centuries earlier God asked Abraham to bring his son Isaac and offer him as a sacrifice and at the last second God stopped him and provided a ram caught in a thicket to be the substitute. (Genesis 22:9-14)

Here on Mt. Moriah, God would once again hold back the hand of death and provide salvation for His people.

David rushed to Ornan. The Jebusite bowed before the King.

> "Then David said to Ornan, 'Give me the site of this threshing floor, that I may build on it an altar to the Lord; for the full price you shall give it to me that the plague may be restrained from the people.'" (I Chron.21:22)

Ornan offered to not only give the King the threshing floor, but everything needed for the offering. (I Chronicles 21:23)

David refused the gift and said:

> *"'No, but I will surely buy it for the full price; for I will not take what is yours for the Lord, or offer a burnt offering which costs me nothing.'" So David gave Ornan 600 sheckels of gold by weight for the site." (I Chronicles 21:24-25)*

David built the altar there. God brings fire from heaven to consume the sacrifice. (I Chronicles 21:26) Trembling and worshipping at the foot of the smoking altar, David understood God's grace more clearly now than at any other time in his life. David said:

> *"This is the house of the Lord God, and this is the altar of burnt offering for Israel." (I Chronicles 22:1)*

This is the place where God's judgment and His mercy will meet for generations to come, where sins will be atoned for and pardons be granted. This was the site where David's son Solomon would build God's Temple. That was the site of the first of millions of sacrifices; the site where the Son of God would come one day and become God's atoning sacrifice for sin on a hill on Mt. Moriah.

This whole episode started with David's sin and ended with God's finger pointing to His mercy extended to sinful men. At Calvary, the judgment which should have fallen on the human race all was poured out on Jesus.

God has the ability to turn cursing into blessing!

George

Chapter 10 - "Don't Mess Up the House... Carol's Coming Home!"

Day 45 – (Day 13 @ Bacharach Institute for Rehabilitation) Tuesday, September 15, 2009

Dr. Alfaro, Carol's doctor at Bacharach, gave me the advice – "Don't mess up the house... your wife is coming home."

CAROL'S COMING HOME – Thursday. No therapy on Thursday – she will be leaving Bacharach in the morning.

She will keep up an outpatient therapy routine starting next week.

Vision – Carol, her PT Anthony and I met with the neuro-ophthalmologist today. Dr. Rummel verified field cuts to the bottom right, an inability to point her eyes and stay focused on objects and depth perception issues. He said the good news is that everything she has is treatable – she must start therapies that force her eyes to point and focus on objects and when her eyes start to wander – she must try to force herself to bring them back and focus on the object at which she is supposed to be looking.

Physical Therapy – Carol is walking normally. We climbed 15 steps to go to the neuro-ophthalmologist visit on the second floor. She walked on a treadmill for 30 minutes and rode on an exercise bike that included pushing and pulling her arms for 15 minutes. It was a strenuous workout.

Occupational Therapy – She is doing more of the day-to day things she will have to do when she gets home. Her occupational therapist, Allen, did vision exercises that will help Carol point her eyes and focus on objects.

Appointments scheduled - Dr. Bell (Neurologist) at Jefferson Wednesday – September 23; CT Scan at Jefferson Neuroscience Hospital on Thursday, September 24 at 11:00 a.m.; and Dr. Rummel (Neuro-Ophthalmologist) at Bacharach on October 20..

Morning Thoughts – September 15, 2009

Neurons work by using a combination of electrical and chemical impulses. Inside the neuron, the signal is electrical. How fast does that signal travel through the nerve? The speed is almost the speed of light, 186,000 miles per second or seven times around the earth in one second. Electricity travels through a material depending on the conductivity of the material so the speed is slightly less than "c".

But where one nerve connects with its neighbor, in a connection called the synapse, the signal switches to a chemical message. This chemical signal must be ferried across the synapse by a chemical known as a neurotransmitter. There are more than one hundred different neurotransmitters, including such popular names as serotonin and dopamine. This splash of a chemical signal across the synapse is slow in comparison to the electrical impulse traveling through the nerve.

Dr. Swenson writes, "Think of it this way – you are speeding on an open road like Steve McQueen in a Hollywood chase scene and you come to a river that has no bridge and you have to park there and wait for the next ferry to carry you across. When you get to the other side you jump in, hit the gas and fly off again until you reach the next river and have to wait there for another ferry. That's the way neural messages pass from one nerve cell to the next on their way to the brain.

How long does a signal take from sensory cell to the brain? A few thousandths of a second – but most of that time is taken 'waiting for ferries'."

The electrical activity of the brain not only receives and generates currents running up and down through the neurons; it is also responsible for brain waves. A tracing of brain waves is done by an EEG (Electroencephalogram) by placing electrodes on various parts of the scalp and recording what comes through from the brain. Carol had this done at Jefferson in her first week. It took her friend, Debbie, four hours one night to pick the glue out of Carol's hair. This test showed Carol's brain was functioning at a high level.

The brain produces four types of waves that are measured on an EEG – 1) Alpha Waves (waves seen more when we are relaxed but aware), 2) Beta Waves (waves seen more when we are fully alert), 3) Delta Waves (waves seen more when we are sleeping) and 4) Theta Waves (waves seen more when we are drowsy) Brain researchers are working with patients who are totally paralyzed to determine if a computer assembled listing of electrical potentials in the brain waves could suggest what a paralyzed person is thinking at different times of a day. The device they are trying to develop will be like a "thought translation device". Amazing.

The Scripture says,

> *"You perceive my thoughts from afar – before a word is on my tongue you know it completely, O LORD." (Psalm 139:2,4)*

Before my brain starts resonating those alpha through theta waves, God knows my thought. Now that is illuminating – the God who made my nerves

120

and my brain also knows my thoughts before I think them. That certainly qualifies as awesome!

*(Resource – **More Than Meets the Eye**, Richard Swenson, Navpress, Colorado Springs 2000)*

George

Day 46 – (Day 14 @ BIR – Bacharach Institute for Rehab. – Day 1 @ Home) Wednesday, September 16, 2009

CAROL'S COMING HOME – Today. No therapy, she will be leaving Bacharach after breakfast.

She will keep up an outpatient therapy routine starting next week.

Vision – Carol, her PT Anthony and I met with the neuro-ophthalmologist today. Dr. Rummel verified field cuts to the bottom right, a lack of ability to point her eyes and stay focused on objects and depth perception issues. He said the good news is that everything she has is treatable – she must start therapies that force her eyes to point and focus on objects and when her eyes want to start wandering – she has to try to force herself to bring them back and focus on the object at which she is supposed to be looking.

Physical Therapy – Along with her walking, the PT's had Carol climb a step ladder today.

Occupational Therapy – She is doing more of the day-to day things she will have to do when she gets home. Her OT, Allen, did vision exercises

121

with Carol to point her eyes and focus on objects.
Allen also had Carol fry an egg.

George

Morning Thoughts – September 16, 2009

Yesterday we thought about the four types of waves that are measured on an EEG – (1) Alpha Waves (waves seen more when we are relaxed but aware), (2) Beta Waves (waves seen more when we are fully alert), (3) Delta Waves (waves seen more when we are sleeping) and (4) Theta Waves (waves seen more when we are drowsy) We also talked about brain researchers who are working with patients who are totally paralyzed to determine if a computer assembled listing of electrical potentials in the brain waves could suggest what a paralyzed person is thinking at different times of a day. The device they are trying to develop will be like a "thought translation device".

We pointed out the Scripture that says:

> *"You perceive my thoughts from afar – before a word is on my tongue you know it completely, O LORD." (Ps.139:2,4)*

Before my brain starts resonating those alpha through theta waves, God knows my thoughts. Now that is amazing – the God who made my nerves and my brain also knows my thoughts before I think them.

What does this imply about our worship? God understands what is happening in my heart and mind when I worship Him. Medical professionals have long chronicled the positive effects of faith on healing and recovery times in hospitals. There is an interesting nexus where science and faith meet. It is as if the cold, number-driven, scientifically-oriented doctors are begrudgingly forced to admit that faith is good medicine - an interesting, though pragmatic, surrender.

Now I am not saying that you can spot the Holy Spirit on a brain scan. A God great enough to create life can remain un-scan-able until He chooses to reveal Himself. His presence and His design are clearly seen in the world around us. The intelligence of design in your thumb is enough to understand there is a grand design around us... which suggests a Grand Designer. Only fools deny this. I do believe we can see His impact in people's lives too. That God loves Carol is being shouted every day to anyone who has ears to hear.

Here's how the Apostle Paul put it:

> *"For the invisible things of Him from the creation of the world are clearly seen, being understood by the things that are made, even His Eternal Power and Godhead, so that they (the human race) are without excuse." (Romans 1:20)*

And David wrote,

> *"All Thy works shall praise Thee, O LORD; and Thy saints shall bless Thee." (Psalm 145:10)*

*(Resource – **More Than Meets the Eye**, Richard Swenson, Navpress, Colorado Springs 2000)*

George

I had dreamed of coming home since I was cognizant enough to realize I was in the hospital. Now that the possibility was becoming a reality, I was ecstatic! However, as appealing as the idea of sleeping in my own bed, next to my dear husband, with Ashley at our feet was, it was also paralyzingly frightening. Up to this point, dressing unaided, washing unaided, walking unaided, eating unaided were my goals.

From this day forward, there would be no hospital bed, no medication nurse, no physical therapist, no meal service. From now on reading Dr. Seuss and other children's books would not occupy my days; choosing a greeting card from the hospital gift shop and attempting to return it to its correct location in the display would not consume my time. I would be home, in my home, but I was not me. I remember lying in bed that evening after George left and realizing I could not visualize how I would, or if I would ever resume being me. As melodramatic as that may sound, I would, over the next few months, come to terms with what made Carol R. Quinn, Carol R. Quinn.

Carol

Morning Thoughts – September 17, 2009

I enjoy this devotional thought from one of my favorite authors, Vance Havner. Vance writes…

> *"Lord, You have been our dwelling place in all generations." (Ps.90:1)*

God is not only our hiding place, He is our dwelling place. He is not merely a Shelter for the night, He is our Staying Place forever. There we are not in hiding, we are at home.

Some flee to Him for refuge but do not make themselves at home. They worry and doubt and fear.

The Israelite who worried although the blood was on his doorpost was just as safe as the one who rested in peace, but he was not enjoying his security.

Blessed is the soul who learns how to nestle down deep and snug in his Abiding Place.

We might as well settle down in God now, for the day will come when only God will remain. Our bodies, our homes, our financial security, our jobs, all these house us but temporarily, and one day all of them will fail. We had better be "home in God" now. Then if we lose all else we still have all we ever really had.

Your Hiding Place is your Dwelling Place. Make yourself at home!

*("**Pepper 'n Salt**", Vance Havner. Fleming H. Revell Company, 1966)*

George

Chapter 11 – Faith Becomes Sight

As I write this chapter, I fervently wish George had kept a journal for a longer period, for he is a better observer of what happened, as you can tell from his journal entries. How he was able to keep the journal, take care of me, the house, the dog, and remain sane is a testimony to his faith, love, and the incalculable acts of kindness and prayers of family, friends. Now that I am home, it is less travel for him, but, I fear, far more responsibility.

The first few days at home are a blur for me. The one thing I vividly remember is the first Sunday home. George helped me choose an outfit to wear to church. While that seems like a simple sentence, the task was much more involved. I had not seen my dress clothes for over a month. My closet is a walk-in, but due to my pack-rat tendencies, you cannot actually walk in it . . . the floor is covered with items that, to this day eight years later, remain. We eventually found an outfit, shoes, the whole nine yards.

We attended church. The love of my church family was overwhelming. We returned home, undressed, and George decided to make a quick run to the grocery store. He carefully placed me in our recliner, reclined it fully, put on a movie, assured me he would be home in a snap, handed me the remote and left.

This was the first time I had been alone for quite some time. It was disquieting, but somewhat exciting. I was independent, I was on my own, I was in control. I reached for the remote to lower the volume on the television. I could not see any of the buttons. I pressed what I thought was the volume control, but alas, it was the channel control. The next thing I knew, a robust Italian woman with an equally robust voice was belting out an Italian aria.

I fumbled for the remote only to hear it hit the floor. I reached for the recliner handle only to find I could not find it! So, when George returned home some 30 minutes later, he found me fully reclined, aria blaring, and hysterically crying. This recovery was going to be more of a challenge than I had anticipated, that was for sure!!

Suffice it to say, each day, really each hour, brought new challenges. I will not bore you with every detail but will mention a few episodes. I do this in keeping with the reasons we wrote this book, to encourage anyone who may suffer an incident similar to mine and to glorify the God who restored me.

As previously mentioned, George had returned to work for the first day of school. He was able to return full time not long after my returning home and beginning therapy as an outpatient. As everyone knows who teaches or has children, shortly after school resumes in the fall, Back to School Night is scheduled. While George insisted it would not be a problem for him to miss it this year, I knew he prepared a special show for his physics classes parents involving a motion sensor, computer interface, projector and a falling basketball to measure the acceleration due to gravity. So as insistent as he was that he could stay home, I was equally insistent that he attend. I won!

While I had become accustomed to being home during the day... accustomed is such a strong word. While I had adjusted to George finding clothes; having George help me dress; having George tie my shoes; sitting on the couch until my sister-in-law, Carol arrived to pick me up; exiting the house via the garage because I could not maneuver the three front steps; having Carol drop me off in front of the rehab center; spending time in therapy; having Carol come into rehab because I could not find her car; going to lunch with Carol, a true blessing; returning home; entering the house via the garage and collapsing onto the couch as if I had just scaled Everest. If you can call that accustomed! So, while I had become "accustomed" to being home during the day, spending the night alone was a whole different ball game. Our dear friend Pam gladly offered to spend the evening with me while George went to introduce his students' parents to the wonderful world of physics. All started out well. George had cooked dinner, cleaned up afterwards, gotten dressed and left. Pam arrived shortly thereafter. We sat and talked for quite some time, catching up on things since I had been hospitalized. As we sat, the sun began to set. Pam asked where the light switch was. For the life of me, I could not remember! Of course, I have no table lamps! We had been in our home for two years, and obviously I had turned on the lights before, but this was one of the many things that was gone from my memory. Poor Pam! She did not want to insult me but did not want to sit in the dark all evening either. We finally found the light switch for the kitchen.. . good enough! When George returned home, he reacquainted me with the location!. In my defense, and Pam's, it was somewhat behind my 10-foot potted palm!

One of the most challenging and most rewarding experiences in my recovery was outpatient therapy. At first, my sister-in-law, Carol, brought me three days a week to Betty Bacharach Rehabilitation Center. I worked with a multitude of therapists, but one, Claire, took me under her wing. I met her briefly during inpatient therapy and I believe she was intrigued by my case. She and all the therapists at Bacharach are in the business of restoring lives. I am eternally grateful to all of them!

Therapy is NOT for sissies! Hours upon hours spent attempting to assemble jigsaw puzzles, EIGHT PIECE puzzles. Reading words in HUGE fonts letter by letter.

130

Attempting to recreate a pattern from a picture of push pins, FIVE push pins! Reading children's books, DR. SEUSS! Twice a day vision therapy on a computer-generated program. Learning to write again! We are fearfully and wonderfully made as the Lord tells us. As I began to realize the depth of my deficits, I realized the magnitude of the One who created me. My identity did not lie in my ability to DO anything! My identity lay in my relationship to MY Savior. Yes, the Carol R. Quinn who entered the hospital in July might never be seen again. But the one who emerged would know who she truly was, a child of the King!

Carol

A Letter from Roseann Stollenwerk – Roseann and Carol carpooled back and forth to their jobs at Stockton University. Over the years they have become the best of friends. They resumed commuting together as Carol returned to work.

Where do I begin? I can't even describe how I felt when I received the news about Carol (my best friend, my sister). I remember George calling me with the news, my heart sank! I felt so hopeless… lost.

When I visited Carol in the hospital shortly after her injury, I remember her laying there not being able to see, or remember things, not able to move and being afraid.

Carol had a long road to recovery ahead of her, and she had the best support system anyone could ask for. To watch her each day get herself up (with George's help), get dressed and start her day with therapy was amazing. She had her good days and bad days, but who wouldn't? She didn't let this drag her down.

131

Carol is our miracle from God! He was not finished with her. Carol has many who will seek her advice, and turn to her when they have a problem. She is honest and trustworthy. She has a heart of gold. Carol loves the Lord and her husband with all her heart and soul, and of course Carol loves animals, especially horses, dolphins and dogs. Who could not love Carol R. Quinn?

As part of therapy for Carol, my seven year old daughter, Kaitlyn, and I would play games with her. Kaitlyn and Carol would read her children's book together.

Now it was time to head back to work. The Lord had a big hand in all of this. A deeper friendship than anyone could imagine blossomed between Carol, George and myself. Since we live near each other and Carol could not drive any longer by herself, I became Carol's chauffeur, and off to work we headed. Each day I took Carol to work, therapy and back home. I had the honor of watching Carol's amazing improvement, and I believe this kept her going. Having the interactions with the students was also therapy for her. I believe that going back to work gave her a reason to push herself to her fullest potential and made her recovery quicker. It also took her mind off of herself and self-pity. Going back to work was the best medicine for Carol.

On occasion, Carol would drive to work. She was determined to be able to drive herself somewhere, especially to help George if there was an emergency. She has some quirks with remembering her right from her left. Carol would be driving and at times would either hug the left side or the right side of the road. I would say "Carol, move to your right!" Carol would go towards her left, and I would say "your other right," and we would laugh. Carol is not good with change, especially when it comes to driving, LOL. Another favorite memory of mine

132

with Carol is when we had to take a detour through Mays Landing and cross over at the bulk head. I rolled down my window and Carol said "what are you doing?" I said, "rolling my window down in case we end up in the water, so I can get out." We laughed all the way home. I could go on and on with stories.

Carol conquered! She is an amazing women, wife, sister, aunt, and friend. I love Carol to the moon and back, and I'm so grateful and blessed to have her and George in my life. God is good and has been with Carol every step of the way.

Love,
Roseann Stollenwerk

There was one more incident of note in early 2010. We did have a setback. Carol had been weaned off her anti-seizure medicine, Keppra. I decided to treat Carol to a needed Valentine's trip to Disney World. That was always a fun destination for Carol since the park's opening in 1971 at which time Carol and her college friends made their first trip to see Mickey. We flew down and were booked in the Polynesian Village. We had a great time, saw the fireworks, had lunch in Prince Stephen's dining room in the castle and swam with dolphins. On the last day after our bags were all packed and we were waiting for the transport to the airport, Carol had a seizure. The EMTs came in and measured Carol's vitals. Carol was not fully aware of her surroundings. The ambulance sped her to the Dr. P. Phillips Hospital in Orlando. We stayed there for several days of new meds and observation.

My brother John, ever the pragmatic one, suggested that we not fly home, since plane flights were part of the August and now February neurological events. As he said, "Why take a chance?" We spoke to our friend, DJ and he insisted on driving from New Jersey down to Florida to pick us up. We agreed and waited for him to arrive in Orlando. In the meantime, Carol's brother Ronnie and his wife Gail, drove across the state from Bradenton to visit his Lil' Sis'. When Ronnie arrived, Carol was asleep in her hospital bed and Ronnie said to me, "She is so beautiful; she reminds me so much of my grand mom Mammie." Carol was heavily sedated. The doctors decided to give her two different anti-seizure meds for the ride home to ensure that the ride would be seizure-free. The meds were Dilantin and Phenobarbital.

DJ arrived and we started our slow ride back to New Jersey. Carol was really zonked out from exhaustion and all the meds… so DJ and I had plenty of time to talk on the way home. Our friends, Joe and Laura, in Sumter, South Carolina put us up for rest stop on the way home. Laura and I helped Carol get in the shower in the morning before we resumed our trek home.

We got back to New Jersey and set an appointment at Jefferson. They examined Carol and scaled back some of the anti-seizure medicine. We eventually tried to wean Carol off all her anti-seizure meds again and she had a couple more seizures. So the doctors and we eventually decided to keep Carol on a prophylactic maintenance dose Keppra, 500 mg twice a day to

guard against her having any more seizure
episodes.

George

Day 264 – (Day 219 @ Home) Thursday, April 22, 2010

Therapy

Carol is being weaned off of the Dilantin she
started taking after her seizure in Florida – she is
going to stay on the Keppra. The one side-effect of
the Keppra is that it makes patients depressed and
open to big mood swings.

We have many down moments, but her vision is a
lot better. In fact, she's seeing better than she did
when we left for Florida. Thank the Lord.

Carol has returned to work. She works
Wednesday, Thursday and Friday. She is doing
Vision Restoration Therapy at home and on
Mondays, Wednesdays and Fridays, Carol has
occupational therapy with Clare at Bacharach.

Friday is Carol's appearance at the Jefferson
Hospital Neurological Grand Round. We will be
meeting Dr. Will Neil at 7:30 AM.

A Grand Round is when the entire Jefferson
neurological team convenes to discuss a series of
the most interesting cases with which they have
been dealing. Carol's case is fascinating because
there was no traumatic head blow that began her
series of neurological events. And beyond that,
50% of Sub-Arachnoid Hemorrhages (SAH) result

in death. And then, after surviving the onset, the resulting infarctions left Carol totally blind – now 7 months later she is back to work with virtually 20/20 vision.

It is a miracle… but there are many more miles to travel on the road to recovery. At the same time, we are very thankful for how far she has come.

Thanks for praying!

Chapter 12 - The Grand Round

Day 272 – (Day 227 @ Home) Friday, April 30, 2010

Therapy

Today was Carol's appearance at the Jefferson Hospital Neurological Grand Round. Our friends Frank and Debbie, DJ, John (my brother) and Carol (his wife) came to be part of the day. We met Dr. Will Neil at 7:30 a.m.

The single topic for this month's Grand Round at Jefferson was Carol's case for the whole hour.

Dr. Neil and Dr. DeChant, two of Carol's doctors when she was admitted to the Jefferson Neuroscience Hospital last August, moderated the meeting. Dr. Neil had me read from our chronology of the events starting with when Carol and I were on vacation in Colorado and the events that led up to Carol coming to Jefferson. The morning Carol was admitted to Jefferson, she couldn't put the cap back on her lip-liner and had difficulty reading the scroll that was running on the bottom of the TV and we went to the hospital that sent us to Jefferson.

Neil and DeChant took over the narrative from the day Carol was admitted to the Jefferson Neuroscience Hospital and described how the case proceeded.

Neil and DeChant invited their colleague, Dr. William Young, an expert in the field of head pain, to interview Carol before the gathered department members. Dr. Young was not a member of Carol's original team but had volunteered to interview her

137

when he came to understand the nature of Carol's case. Carol and Dr. Young were seated in front of the auditorium as the neurology department listened. Dr. Young asked Carol about her headaches while in Colorado. Dr. Young probed each headache account for how fast the headache came on, where the pain was located, if the pain got worse as time elapsed and what was the duration of each headache. The first headache (Sunday, August 2nd) was in Rocky Mountain National Park on Trail Ridge Road elevation 12,000 feet. The pain was located on the right side of Carol head without too much pain. Carol took an allergy pill… the headache went away. The second headache (Monday, August 3rd) was at the ranch… a piercing headache that lasted all night. Tuesday – we went to the Timberline Clinic – received a negative CT scan – Carol was diagnosed with altitude sickness – was prescribed a diuretic & stayed in Estes – no additional headaches. The third headache (Wednesday, August 5th) came on all-of-a-sudden as Carol bent over to dry her hair after a shower – this was a sudden-onset – like a thunderclap – the ranch provided a house in Estes (lower elevation, 5800 feet) where we went and Carol was fine. The fourth headache (Thursday, August 6th) had an extended duration, caused us to go down to Ft. Collins (below 5000') where Carol stayed until we flew home.

Carol's doctors went into the details of Carol's 39-day stay at Jefferson, particularly focusing on her first week when Carol lost her sight and presented the serious signs of neurological problems. They described what a difficult time they were having determining exactly what the problem was. We saw a PowerPoint presentation that included Carol's CT, MRI, CT Angiogram slides of her first week. They showed her original brain bleed, which was small, and her significant constriction of vascular pathways that was the cause of so much concern. We saw, in graphic relief, why the team had such a hard time identifying and diagnosing Carol's problem. Their differential diagnosis included several possibilities including vasculitis, an auto-immune problem and reversible cerebral vasoconstriction syndrome. The team eventually ruled out all others except RCVS.

Dr. Neil showed a videotape he and Dr. Urtecho took of Carol around Day 38 of her stay – which showed how hard a time Carol was still having after 7 weeks of recovery. I think that was eye-opening for Carol to see how bad it was. She doesn't remember that time very well.

Dr. Neil went through a survey of journal articles related to RCVS and any connections to high altitude activities.

The neurologists in the auditorium asked a slew of questions. Most of them revolved around options that were or were not considered in determining Carol's diagnosis. Drs. Neil and DeChant answered all questions.

Dr. Young concluded that Carol probably started out with altitude sickness that may have initiated the RCVS even when Carol was in Colorado. He said that when Carol flew back to Philadelphia and came home, the symptoms had not become serious, but the next morning the constriction was getting worse evidenced in her inability to put the cap on her lip-liner and follow the scroll across the bottom of the screen on a news channel. When she came to Jefferson, even though the bleed wasn't serious, Dr. Young concluded, the constriction was rapidly making her condition worse. The therapy to keep her blood pressure elevated allowed the blood to flow through the constricted vessels limiting further brain injury until the RCVS ran its course.

Dr. Neil told us that RCVS was first isolated and documented in the 1980s – so they have only known about this syndrome for about the last thirty years.

Carol wanted to do this Grand Round to help doctors treat any future patients who might suffer from a similar condition. She was strong and courageous. I think this meeting helped her too. She sometimes gets frustrated with her lack of progress, but really when she gets a fuller picture of how far she has come with God's help and the help of these doctors, she can't help but appreciate how blessed she really is.

Several doctors, who treated Carol at various points of her stay, came up after the program to tell her how glad they were to see her doing so well. It was a good day!

Thanks for praying!

A Footnote to the Grand Round

In early 2011, an article was published in the journal "Neurology" written by Carol's doctors: Dr. Will Neil, Dr. Valerie DeChant and Dr. Jackie

Urtecho. The title of that article… **"Pearls and Oysters: Reversible Cerebral Vasoconstriction Syndrome Precipitated by Ascent to High Altitude"**, _Neurology_, Vol.76, Issue 2, January 11, 2011. Carol's hope to have her case written up so that it may help others in a similar situation has become reality.

George

Day 295 – (Day 250 @ Home) Saturday, May 22, 2010

Therapy

Carol is taking Keppra as an anti-seizure med. It has side effects of depression and mood swings. She has not had a seizure since that one in Florida. Thank the Lord.

Carol is working five days a week and doing Vision Restoration Therapy at home. Her occupational therapy with Clare at Bacharach has ended. Her vision is a lot better – her reading and writing are also better.

This Sunday I will be sharing Carol's story at church – it is a story of God's grace and a profile in courage on Carol's part.

Please pray!

George

One Year – Monday, August 2, 2010

Therapy

Carol is still on Keppra, the anti-seizure med. Her
vision is good – she still has a small field cut. Last
night she read a whole chapter out of her book,
"Having a Mary Heart in a Martha World". She's
reading that book in preparation for a Women's
Bible study she has Thursday night.

George

I must interject at this point in George's narrative. When
he says I "read" a book, I want to clarify what that meant
at this point in my recovery. I do this for any reader who
may be attempting to recover from a brain injury. My
reading the book entailed a friend, Sandy, from church
typing out the parts of the book we were studying that
week in a LARGE print along with the questions that
accompanied the chapter; sitting with George and reading
the material. I then attempted to write out the answers
with George's help. Repeating this process for each
chapter of the book; progress is sometimes slow, but it is
progress.

If you are reading this and can effortlessly read and write,
thank the Lord. If you are reading this the way I did, thank
the Lord for husbands and friends and therapists. If you
cannot read this, stick with your therapy and thank the
Lord for His unfailing grace!

Carol

We went to Florida for vacation by car. Carol's
sister Evelyn went with us – we stopped in South
Carolina again to see our friends, Joe & Laura
Palmer. No problems – we had a great time. Carol

caught up with her brother, Ronnie and his wife Gail and her nephews Ronnie and Jeff.

Carol is working every day and may be up for a promotion – no surprise. She drove to church Sunday night – Thanks be to God.

Please keep praying!

Our dear friend, Rosemarie Bellace, owns a driving school. Rose has taken the job of helping Carol feel comfortable behind the wheel again. It has been a blessing catching up with Rose and seeing her skill assisting Carol with parking and driving again. Thank you Rosie!

George

When I first left the hospital and began in-patient rehabilitation, finishing rehab was my ultimate goal. Once home, finishing out-patient rehabilitation and returning to work became my prime objectives.

Once back to work, being useful to my students occupied my mind. Once that was accomplished, my desire to be useful at home and resume our life pre-brain injury was my goal.

Throughout these days, weeks, and months, each small victory was a milestone. When I was struggling to remember how to hook a bra and dress myself, driving was not even a blip on my radar.

However, as I continued therapy and continued to improve, driving became an option and one I truly wished to resume. Enter Dr. Rosemarie Bellace! Dear friend

143

from college, traveling buddy, educator, basketball coach, devoted daughter, and believe it or not, driving instructor! Rosie was one of my ten bridesmaids. We had laughed ourselves simple more times than I can recount during and following our college days. We had kept in touch, but slowly drifted apart. However, when she heard of my situation, she was there in a heartbeat!

George and Rosie turned our garage into a safe space by painting yellow lines on each side to guide me in, placing red cones with yellow flags to stop me from driving out the back of the building, and recreating a parallel parking test in our driveway.

I had asked the Lord to allow me to learn to drive again. George had suffered a heart attack in 2004, and my prayer was to allow me to recover enough to be able to get back and forth to the hospital if I needed to.

Once again, the Lord was there ahead of the request. Who knew I would need a friend to assist me with the monumental task of learning how to drive again? Who knew a friend from college would retire from teaching and open a driving school? Who knew that friend would drop everything and come to my aid? The God who knows all! The God who loves me enough to send His son to die for me! The God who loves each of you reading these words with that same amazing love!

Carol

One final comment to give our readers the scope of Carol's rehabilitation... After Carol's brain injury, she virtually had to relearn every life skill again - standing, walking, climbing, feeding herself, dressing herself, reading, writing, typing, etc. In fact, the only habit she seemed to pick up and do naturally was brushing her teeth! Because of her determination and her therapists' resourcefulness, the results were nothing short of marvelous.

George

George's sister, Madeline, contributed this...

Thank you so much for including me in this special list. Being far away while you were facing such enormous challenges was hard for us. The strong faith you relied upon as you struggled through the process of understanding, dealing with, and overcoming this injury was truly inspirational to both of us.

Mike (Madeline's husband) wanted you to know that he asked Saint Pius X Catholic Church in Pretoria, South Africa, to put you on its prayer list. It was during this time that we started going every week to the Catholic church two blocks away from us, and Mike started taking training for Confirmation with a wise old Irish priest named Father Hyacinth (Father Hi, for short).

Worried about Carol, my prayers became more focused, and I even went to confession for the first time in almost 40 years (after 2 unsuccessful tries I just left the church--- either from fear of God or claustrophobia). It's a wonder the little church didn't fall down on my head. Anyway, we were praying when Carol was sick. Hope it helped a little.

Love,
Maddy

Pam Kennedy, a writing professor who worked with Carol at Stockton University...

*I am delighted to participate in this important project.
Here's what I recall from 6 years ago.*

*I remember getting word from your friends and co-workers
that you had suffered a stroke-like brain injury and your
work future was uncertain. From what I understood your
vision was your most problematic issue at that point. Your
days driving that big white Hummer might be over. (The
Prius driver in me thought that might be the work of God
right there – smiley face icon). I remember you coming
back to work and showing courage and humility, and you
commented that perhaps you would be more empathetic
to the needs of your students with disabilities now that you
were struggling with a new normal. As ever, you were
cheerful and self-effacing. I recall one day we were in
your old office in the West Quad building and you needed
to look something up on the computer and you moved
aside to let me and the student work the keyboard. I
remember this because I wasn't sure I did the right thing
by taking over; I didn't want you to feel self-conscious or
inadequate. I know those first few weeks back were
difficult for you, as you struggled to do things that were
once easy. You joked about your brain not working as
well as it used to, and I joked along, too, but I worried that
you were using humor to mask real fear or sadness. Fran
Bottone, that wise woman, knew you would need time.
With time, you adjusted to your post-injury reality and got
back to your job of helping students. Carol, you and I
have teamed up to work with some of the most
challenging students who have ever attended Stockton.*

*You have always handled yourself with good humor and
kindness. Nothing about your approach to your work
changed following your injury; always kind and, always
focused on the students' needs. We miss you a lot*

around here in J-wing, and if retirement doesn't suit you, you can always come back.

All the best,
Pam

One of our favorite pastors is Pastor Matt Chandler from the Village Church in Dallas, Texas. Matt, in his series on Psalm 119, was sharing about the Lord being our portion...

The Lord is my portion; I have promised to keep Your words. I sought Your favor with all my heart; be gracious to me according to Your word. I considered my ways and turned my feet to Your testimonies. (Psalm 119:57-59)

Matt said,

"When I read about God's faithfulness to his people in the Word, I don't want to run from Him when I'm hurting but I want to run towards him."

That really has been our testimony. As we have gone through our ordeal, mainly in 2009, we found that our feet were turned "to His testimonies".

George

Epilogue

As we write the final word of this book, I cannot believe it has been nearly 10 years since the injury occurred and seven since we began to work on this manuscript! I can drive but do so sparingly and most often never alone. I have retired from my work at Stockton University and George has retired from his teaching position. He is one of the pastors at Friendship Bible Church and we are both active in its operation.

You would imagine with a story such as ours and our strong faith in God, we would not be prone to petty squabbles, wasted energy, or repeated failures . . .oh how I wish I could say that was the case!

We, like the children of Israel, have short term memory when it comes to God's faithfulness. However, God is infinite in mercy and does not forget His own!

Our intention in writing this book was to glorify God and, hopefully, encourage or inspire anyone who is struggling with their place in this world. If you know Jesus Christ as Savior, be assured, you are exactly where you are supposed to be, even if you are blind or bedridden. Lean on Him, trust His word, and claim His precious promises. If you do not know Christ as your Savior, perhaps that is why you are reading this story. The Lord is ready, willing and waiting for you to ask Him for forgiveness and place your trust and your future in His hands. Thank you for reading our story.